Growing Grass the Natural Way

ORGANIC LAWN CARE

HOWARD GARRETT

"The Dirt Doctor"

University of Texas Press ⟵⟶ Austin

Unless otherwise noted, all photos are by the author.

Requests for permission to reproduce material from this work should be sent to:
    Permissions
    University of Texas Press
    P.O. Box 7819
    Austin, TX 78713-7819
    http://utpress.utexas.edu/about/book-permissions

♾ The paper used in this book meets the minimum requirements of
ANSI/NISO Z39.48-1992 (R1997) (Permanence of Paper).

Library of Congress Cataloging-in-Publication Data

Garrett, Howard, 1947–
    Organic lawn care : growing grass the natural way / by Howard Garrett "The Dirt
Doctor." — 1st ed.
        p.   cm.
    Includes index.
    ISBN 978-0-292-72849-3 (pbk. : alk. paper)
1. Lawns. 2. Turfgrasses. 3. Organic gardening. I. Title.
    SB433.G36 2014
    635.9'647—dc23   2013030495
    doi:10.7560/728493

Contents

Preface

Americans are a little nutty about their lawns. They love dark green mono-cultures of turfgrasses and literally despise weeds. It's more than just an aesthetic issue—it's emotional. This book is about how to achieve that pristine look but also how to think differently about what is a more practical way to address turfgrass establishment and installation. This book gives readers everything they need to know about successfully growing turfgrass the natural organic way while saving water and money. Whether you are interested in growing a grass for your putting green or having the lowest-maintenance turf possible, I hope you find the information within these pages.

Howard Garrett

Introduction

Environmental Issues

Environmental concern has become mainstream. "Green" has become ubiquitous. Unfortunately, most of the marketing companies using the various "eco-friendly" terms don't have the slightest idea what they are talking about. There is increasing interest from homeowners and businesses to be "green" because that's the "in thing" to do and the "feel good" thing to do. On the other hand, getting back in touch with nature is truly important to more and more people, especially those living in urban situations.

What still surprises many is that the only truly green approach is the natural-organic program for grounds management. Many companies that brag about their LEED (Leadership in Energy and Environmental Design)-certified buildings, for example, still allow the grounds maintenance to be done with synthetic salt fertilizers and toxic chemical pesticides. Some of them realize that reducing water is an important environmental issue, but few of them realize that 40–50 percent of their water bill expenses could be saved by using an organic program. One of the big problems is that the landscape industry continues to tell homeowners and businesses that the organic approach doesn't work. Many universities that prepare those who want to enter the landscape industry are still teaching the use of soil-, air- and water-injuring synthetic fertilizers and toxic chemical pesticides. They go further by proclaiming that organic techniques don't work. But they don't work for these people because they have never tried them.

As a result, maintenance of turf is still basically in the dark ages—the chemical dark ages that is. It all started just after World War II when new uses for weapons were created. Nitrogen started going into fertilizers instead of into bombs, and toxic chemicals started being put into "pest control" canisters. The irony is that these products don't work well, especially in the long term. What the harsh chemicals do that is so bad is destroy the life in the soil.

This book is designed to teach you how to choose the right grasses for the site and situation and also how to use a completely different management approach that protects the life in the soil and improves it to make grass plants healthier and turf management easier and more cost effective. While not as visually impressive as a forest, jungle, or ocean reef, the life at work in a patch of turf can be every bit as interesting—if it is as alive and healthy as it should be.

History of the Lawn

Lawns are thought to be a primarily American landscape feature, even though most of the common lawn grasses are not native to the United States. Lawns have become a big part of our lives and big business. I'm not sure when it all started, but perhaps some king somewhere figured that if he kept the grasses and bushes cut low, he could better see the approaching enemies interested in entering his castle, cutting off his head, and taking his women. Maybe later he discovered that this low-cropped grass looked different and had a nice appearance. As other rich folks noticed and copied this new "refined" look, the lawn was born. Yes, lawns were originally for the wealthy, but now everyone can have their own plot of turf. Colonial Americans apparently surrounded their homes with what was called front meadows or grass yards. George Washington hired English designers and gardeners to create and maintain a bowling green in front of Mount Vernon.

Several organizations are primarily responsible for the popularity of lawns in the United States: the USDA (United States Department of Agriculture), the USGA (United States Golf Association), and the PGA (Professional Golfers' Association of America). These groups have pushed the importance of low-cut, well-maintained monocultures of turfgrass. No part of the landscape has been so advertised and promoted. The USGA and the golf industry have led the charge with the financial support of the chemical industry.

I like to play golf and appreciate the beauty and precise maintenance of the turf on golf courses. However, American golf courses have warped the attitude of homeowners, landscape companies, and turf managers worldwide. One specific golf course is the primary culprit. It is the Augusta National Golf Club where the Masters golf tournament is played. This property has no weeds. It is the ultimate monoculture and the most artificial natural beauty that exists anywhere in the world. Yes, I am as impressed with that golf course as anyone who has ever experienced it, but that doesn't excuse its damage to the environment—and not just to that specific site in Augusta, Georgia, but to home lawns, commercial landscapes, and golf courses worldwide.

When visitors or television viewers first witness the perfection of the turf at Augusta, few realize that the grass is a cool-season variety groomed to be at its peak during the tournament. There is very little play on the course because most members live in other parts of the world, the course is closed six months out of the year, and the maintenance costs of this tract of turf are astronomical.

The average annual cost of golf course maintenance for eighteen holes may be as high as $2 million; at some private country clubs it is $5 million. The annual cost at Augusta National is rumored to be in excess of $20 million. If the real truth were known, the budget is most likely unlimited. And, like most golf courses, it is not under an organic program—quite the contrary. What's wrong with all that you say? Nothing, if they could maintain their artificial setting without influencing so many other people and places.

As of 2013, there are very few totally organic golf courses in the country. The reason? Golf course superintendents do what the USGA, Texas A&M University, and other universities teach them to do. No major universities recommend any organic techniques. Because few of their peers use organic techniques, following the status quo is usually done. If superintendents follow the university-prescribed fertilizer and pest-control instructions—the same ones being used by their fellow superintendents at other clubs around the area as well as around the country—there is a comfort level. It's not a comfort that comes from using the best approach, but a comfort that if failure occurs, "it's not my fault." Turf managers, not just the golf course people, are intimidated to try methods and products that aren't approved by the current conventional wisdom. The status quo is very powerful. When grass fails to perform—even expensive golf greens die—the manager has a convenient out if he has used the highest technology and the conventionally used state-of-the-art products and techniques. If, on the other hand, he has ventured off into the land of the "chemical heretic" and has gone organic, he has no one else to blame. He has to take the responsibility himself.

Tierra Verde, a municipal course in Arlington, Texas, is one of the few courses currently using organic fertilizer practices. They aren't 100 percent organic yet because of the use of herbicides, although they use these at a much lower volume and rate than others do. Totally organic programs work better in every aspect if all the costs are factored in. In 2011, the total annual course maintenance budget of Tierra Verde was $700,000, and that included the cost of water that they have to pay just like everyone else. Under the direction of Eric Johnson, the Rawls Course at Texas Tech University was under a similar natural-organic program and has experienced similar success with cost savings and quality of turf. The only other golf course using organic techniques, that I know of, is the Vineyard Golf Club on Martha's Vineyard. I don't put it in the same category, however, because this place literally has an unlimited budget.

Water Issues

Water is a big issue today, and it will become a bigger issue every year and ultimately the biggest issue, especially in the more arid parts of the country.

Runoff of high-nitrogen synthetic fertilizers and toxic chemical pesticides is a major problem for the health of our water sources and the plant and animal life that depends on them. Without question, the organic approach helps solve this problem. Organic soil amendments and pest-control products not only end the pollution but are the answer to decontaminating the existing problems.

Contamination isn't the biggest problem with water. Having enough water is a more serious issue. One of the most important aspects of changing direction with management practices from synthetic to natural organic is the resulting water savings.

Besides changing management techniques, switching to multispecies turf is one more answer. Not that monoculture turfgrass plantings won't continue to be desired, installed, and maintained, it's just that there is a practical alternative for most people and places. Multispecies turf means just that: many species of grasses and forbs growing together. The overall look is green and very pleasant. Without looking closely, the difference is largely undetectable. Trying to kill the invading species of grass is a silly thing. Why not let the grasses that want to grow, grow? One alleged weed that I often encourage is white clover. I actually plant it in some cases. The tiny black seeds germinate easily when planted late summer to early fall.

> Lawns become increasingly artificial and unnatural in direct proportion to the sales of synthetic lawn-care products.

Organic Approach versus Conventional Approach

The differences between organic and chemical lawn care are considerable. The latter involves ignoring nature's systems and force-feeding the plants with high-nitrogen, highly water-soluble synthetic fertilizers and spraying toxic chemical pesticides on the insect and disease outbreaks that are directly related to the poor fertilization program. The organic method, on the other hand, looks at the soil to determine its condition and then adjusts the balance of chemistry, biology, and physics. The organic gardener or lawn-care professional feeds the living organisms in the soil and lets the healthy soil feed the plants.

The watering schedule is critical to organic lawn care. The most common mistake is watering too often and not deep enough at each watering. The result is weak, shallow root systems and the wasteful use of too much water. Watering less often and deeper each time prevents salt buildup; limits waste from evaporation; and encourages larger, healthier root systems. Putting down about one inch at each watering is a good basic starting point. As with nature, organic programs are dynamic and need to be adjusted from time to time.

Grass clippings and bagged leaves should not be accepted at city landfills. This practice should *never* be allowed so homeowners will use these valuable resources.

An organic turf program will give you not only a beautiful lawn but also a comfortable place where your pets and children can play safely. Synthetically maintained turf really doesn't.

The first thing I always tell people who are considering the organic approach is to get rid of the grass catcher. There are several reasons why grass clippings should be left on the lawn, and there are even stronger arguments for not putting clippings in plastic or paper bags and leaving them on the street curb for the garbage collectors to pick up and haul to the landfill. Clippings provide the critical organic material that beneficial microorganisms in the soil need to create natural fertilizer. In addition, grass clippings contain nutrients, and a large percentage of those nutrients accumulate in the leaf tips, which, of course, is the part that is cut away. University studies have shown that nitrogen in grass clippings left on the lawn can be absorbed back into the living grass plants in less than a week. If you mow your own lawn, you should stop spending the money, time, and energy required to bag the grass clippings. Grass clippings should never be caught, with the exception of immediately before overseeding with cool-season grasses such as rye.

Many cities in this country have a serious problem with the amount of available land left for landfills and garbage dumps. As much as 40 percent of landfill volume is attributed to grass clippings, leaves, and tree chips. Grass makes up a great percentage of all the vegetative materials, and the plastic bags are another

Mulching mowers should be used in turf and on hard surfaces.

serious environmental concern. The fact that this problem even exists is ridiculous because the clippings are beneficial to turf and should be left on the ground. Some experts say that the mowing frequency needs to be increased to once every five days instead of once a week, but I don't agree. In most cases, when organic fertilizers are used and used properly, the grass will be healthy and green but slower growing. Organically maintained turf doesn't have the spurts of growth that are commonly caused by high-nitrogen salt fertilizers. Mowing more often for a special look is okay if time and the budget allow it. An extra mowing may sometimes be needed after a rain because of the extra nitrogen and oxygen that is produced in a thunderstorm.

If excess grass clippings accumulate for whatever reason, put them in the compost pile, not in garbage bags. If you own a mulching mower, you never have to worry about excess clippings because they are ground into fine particles that don't accumulate on the surface because they are eaten quickly by the beneficial soil organisms.

No, leaving the clippings on the lawn does not cause thatch buildup. Just the opposite, in fact—the clippings, along with organic fertilizers, provide food for the microorganisms and naturally slow-release fertilizer nutrients for the grass. Synthetic fertilizers and pesticides kill the microorganisms, causing the thatch to remain and become a problem.

Organic fertilizers, and even the "bridge" products that are sometimes used during the transition stage, don't have to be applied as often. That fact, along with the reduction of insects and diseases, is part of the reason why the organic program is cost effective and in the long term can save a lot of money. Using organic fertilizers and programs that cost more money than the synthetic approach doesn't make any sense. Some proponents and even some organic fertilizer manufacturers don't actually get it. They preach that the natural products cost more and don't work as fast or as well, but it's worth it for the environment. It's doing the right thing that's important. That's malarkey! Those people just don't know what they are doing. To me, if the organic program doesn't work from all aspects, including the financial one, it doesn't work at all and shouldn't be used. A properly designed and executed organic program does work better— in every way.

ORGANIC LAWN CARE

CHAPTER 1

Soil

Soil is a complex mixture of organic and inorganic materials. It consists of air, water, minerals, organic matter, and living organisms. It serves as the source of the water, nutrients, and energy needed for the growth of all plants, including turfgrasses. To have balanced, healthy soil, the physics, biology, and chemistry must all be in order. If they're not, those things can be fixed with natural-organic techniques and products.

Physics (Structure of Soil)

Soil is made up partly of minerals called sand, silt, and clay, and the difference between these three is both physical and chemical. Physically, they are different in size. When soil is tested, how much sand, silt, and clay it contains is determined by using a set of sieves. The resulting percentages place the soil in what is called a soil texture group, such as loam, clay loam, or sandy loam. For example, if a soil contains about 50 percent sand, 30 percent silt, and 20 percent clay, it's called a loam. Clay loam has about 20 percent sand, 20 percent silt, and 60 percent clay. The percentages of these three ingredients will vary for sandy loam, but equal amounts of each is common. Most consider a sandy loam to be the best soil texture for a lawn because it has both good drainage and good nutrient-holding characteristics.

The most important direct effects soil structure has on lawns are the rate at which water enters a particular soil, the amount of water that soil holds, and the rate at which water drains through that soil. As the percentage of sand in a soil increases, water will enter it more quickly, it will hold less water, and the water will move down through the soil faster.

Thus, sandy soils tend to be droughty, and the plants growing in them must be watered more often. Clay soils dramatically slow down water infiltration and increase water retention. Thus, they can be poorly drained and even waterlogged after heavy rains or improper irrigation. Generally, turfgrasses form deeper roots in sandy-type soils than they do in high-clay soils.

Core aeration is very helpful at the beginning of a project.

Physical Soil Modification

The goal of physically modifying a soil is to provide oxygen for soil life—the biology of the system. Microbe health will improve the chemistry and the physics of the soil. All three result in better internal drainage, better aeration, and better root growth. The most commonly used material to improve drainage is sand, but it doesn't help much at all because you can't really change the structure of soil. You can make it better, but sandy soils will always be sandy, loam soils will always be loamy, and clay soils will always be clayey. The only sands I recommend are volcanic sands, which are good for their volcanic properties (paramagnetism) rather than their overblown drainage-improving properties.

Plant growth usually isn't very good in compacted soils, so aeration is recommended. There are several ways to aerate the soil. Heavily compacted soil would benefit greatly from core aeration, or "ripping." Ripping the soil is actually more effective at aerating than poking holes but shouldn't be done if trees exist, as the feeder roots would be torn. The liquid aeration treatment would be to spray or drench the soil with hydrogen peroxide. Applying the 3 percent product from the drug or grocery store is one way to go. Commercial 35 percent hydrogen peroxide is also available and can be mixed at about 1 ounce per gallon of water, but this concentrated product can burn skin and eyes, so it must be handled very carefully. The ideal approach would be to do both. The physically aerated soil lets the liquid penetrate more deeply to help loosen the soil more effectively. Then if you add the Garrett Juice mixture or at least compost tea to the hydrogen peroxide application, you will have fertilized the soil as well as aerated it. All this work is usually a one-time need, unless the soil is physically compacted all over again.

The hydrogen peroxide does kill microbes when it first hits the soil, but that ends fast as it breaks down into water and oxygen. The big positive about the product is that it starts the flocculation of the soil. That means that clumps of soil and air spaces are created. Then the microbes grow back better than ever—especially when organic amendments and fertilizers are used.

Soil can be greatly improved regardless of its color or structure with the addition of organic matter, rock minerals, and sugars. An ideal soil contains about 5 percent organic matter. Most soil before improvement contains less than 1 percent organic matter. Clay soils are actually easier to improve than sandy soils. Clay soils are deficient in air and organic matter. Sandy soils are deficient in everything except sand. Some soils that are high in clay and low in organic matter have very poor drainage. Mixing organic matter into these soils will improve drainage much more so than adding sand. Decomposed or composted organic matter should be used. Fresh organic matter is not as desirable because the organisms that decompose organic matter have a high nitrogen requirement. Thus, any plants growing in soils containing fresh organic matter usually have severe nitrogen draft and deficiencies until the organic matter has decomposed. The most efficient way to improve the physics of the soil in a short time is by mechanical aeration.

Drainage

Soil drainage is an important part of the physics of the soil. Drainage problems can happen not only in heavy clay soils but also in sandy soils. One of the worst drainage problems I have ever encountered was on a residential landscape project that had sandy soil. Everyone on the project was stumped about why the place was a swamp and plants were dying until I had the contractor dig a large hole and we discovered a "hard pan" layer that had apparently been caused by plows moving through the ground at the same depth over and over, year after year when the land was agricultural. Drilling and ripping through this layer so the water wouldn't be trapped solved the problem.

Lack of good soil drainage can be one of the worst continual problems a lawn can have. Grass roots simply won't grow in wet soils. Surface drainage may be adequate if the grade is at least 1 percent. This means that for water to run downhill, the slope should drop at least 1 foot for every 100 feet in distance or ½ foot for every 50 feet from the house.

Riding mowers are not good for poorly drained areas.

While surface drainage is important and will aid greatly in keeping the lawn from becoming waterlogged, especially during periods of heavy rainfall, the internal drainage characteristics of a soil are just as important. Soil may not drain well internally for several reasons. The most common cause is simply the high amount of clay in the soil. Clay holds water, so the higher the percentage of clay in the soil, the more water is held and the poorer the drainage.

Soils that are very high in calcium or sodium may tend to be poorly drained. These are two of the elements that may cause the soil to lose its desirable structure and, thus, its good drainage characteristics. If a soil has lost its structure because it is high in sodium, the addition of gypsum may improve internal drainage. Since gypsum is calcium sulfate, its application to a high-calcium soil won't help in many cases. A soil test will determine if either sodium or calcium is a problem and if gypsum will help. High-calcium soils can be improved with the addition of organic fertilizers, humates, magnesium products and sulfur.

Chemistry (Nutrients of Soil)

The ability of a soil to hold and make nutrients available to a plant depends on the amount of clay and the amount of organic matter it contains. Both the clay particles and the organic matter have a negative charge, and since most plant nutrients have a positive charge, the nutrients are held to their surface for possible future use by the turfgrass plant. Soils very high in sand do not hold many nutrients, so fertilizer programs are more critical. As an extreme example, a lawn grown on a very sandy soil may need to be fertilized with small amounts of fertilizer every two or three weeks, whereas lawns grown on soils containing moderate amounts of clay can go as many as six weeks or more between fertilizer applications. The addition of compost or other forms of organic matter and carbon can help the soil hold water and nutrients, but volcanic rock materials such as lava sand are even more efficient at holding moisture at just the right level for a long time. Sugar can help indirectly by stimulating the growth of microbes. Microbe waste and dead bodies created by their life cycles are the most significant long-term sources of humus in the soil, which has great moisture-holding capacity. These improvements (organic material, rock minerals, and sugar) help keep the proper moisture levels and allow the soil to breathe, which benefits the tilth of the soil. It is all related.

Chemical Soil Modification

The best way to adjust the chemistry of the soil is to take soil samples and send them for testing to a lab that uses the carbon dioxide extraction method, which provides information on what nutrients are available to plants and gives organic recommendations to improve the nutrient availability. One of the few labs that fits that specification is the Texas Plant and Soil Lab (TPSL) in Edinburg, Texas.

The testing lab at Texas A&M is the one most commonly recommended in Texas, but there are other university-related labs around the country. I don't recommend any of them for several reasons, but the main issue is that they use harsh chemicals to do the extraction of the nutrients in soil samples. The A&M lab in the past used the worst techniques. After significant criticism and prodding from those of us in the organic arena (mostly K Chandler, Malcolm Beck, and me), A&M decided to change their testing techniques. Below is the memo that announced the change. It was sent quietly in an attempt to stay under the radar, but we were able to get a copy. The change to a less harsh chemical extractant was a step in the right direction, but the new process (Mehlich III) still doesn't give any useful information about what nutrients are available to the plants.

The Texas Cooperative Extension Soil, Water and Forage Testing Laboratory has changed its primary soil nutrient extractant from the TAMU method (acidified ammonium acetate with EDTA) to the Mehlich III method. The former extractant, originally derived from the Morgan method, underwent multiple changes during its use by the laboratory. Recent research by the laboratory and supporting Extension faculty and staff, Texas Agricultural Experiment Station researchers, agricultural industry, and cooperative agricultural producers indicated the former extractant over-estimated plant-available phosphorus in several isolated agriculturally productive areas of Texas.

A review of historical geological surveys and preliminary research by the Soil, Water and Forage Testing Laboratory suggested the over-estimation of phosphorus in these soils was due to the presence of rock phosphate. Exclusively, the soils of concern are dominated by a high concentration of free-calcium carbonates (pH > 7.6) developed in the Upper Austin Chalk geological deposits. These areas included a narrow band of the soil from North Waco to Oklahoma and along the Rio Grande River.

An exhaustive laboratory research program evaluated each of the major soil nutrient methods used in the south-central United States, along with several others used in North America and one developed by the laboratory. Using field research samples, the following criteria were used in selecting a new test (or maintaining TAMU extract):

1. accuracy in predicting significant economic yield increases to phosphorus fertilization
2. capacity to extract and analyze multiple nutrients
3. ease of use by laboratory
4. use of extractant by neighboring Land-Grant universities
5. relationship between new extractant and TAMU extractant (facilitates use of historic datasets)
6. acceptance by state and federal environmental and agricultural agencies
7. potential acceptance by private laboratories

The only method evaluated that adequately predicted economic yield response to phosphorus fertilization across the numerous research study sites was the Mehlich III extractant. Fortunately, this method currently is being used by Univ. of Arkansas, Oklahoma State Univ., Kansas State Univ., and many private soil-testing laboratories throughout the United States. While published research suggests the Mehlich III extractant also be used for micro-nutrient analysis (iron, zinc, copper and manganese), the Soil, Water and Forage Testing Laboratory did not find a strong enough relationship between existing methodology or plant uptake data to support this claim. The method does however work well for predicting available potassium, calcium, magnesium, sodium and sulfur. Sulfur extracted by the Mehlich III, while strongly correlated with the TAMU method, was significantly lower, and thus existing sulfur recommendations were altered to reflect the difference in sulfur extractability by the methods. The other four elements' recommendations have not been altered at this time.

Impact of Phosphorus Change

Nine hundred eleven soil samples submitted by Texas clientele were analyzed by the laboratory using multiple methodologies, and data was compared to the TAMU method. The only criteria used for selecting these samples were:

1. non-urban samples
2. non-manured samples
3. originated from Texas
4. Non-research samples
5. TAMU phosphorus levels below 200 ppm
6. no apparent issue with salinity
7. soil pH levels between 4.5 and 9.0
8. adequate soil to complete all tests.

Mehlich III data can be used with the following equation to predict EDTA [Ethylenediaminetetraacetic acid] phosphorus levels:

EDTA phosphorus = -40.63 + 4.313*pH*pH + 0.104*M3Mg-0.0000824*M3Mg*M3Mg + 0.718*M3P + 0.00128*M3P*M3P

r = 0.896; P = <0.001

where M3Mg = Mehlich 3 magnesium and M3P = Mehlich 3 phosphorus

All data, except pH, are in ppm or mg/kg. Divide data expressed in lbs./acre by 2 prior to using this equation.

Effectively, soils low in pH (4.5–5.9) will have higher Mehlich III phosphorus levels than the same soils analyzed with the TAMU method. Additionally, soils high in pH will have lower phosphorus levels when analyzed with the Mehlich III [rather] than the TAMU method. These differences have been taken into account by the re-working of the laboratory's phosphorus fertilizer recommendations.

Additional information will be posted in the near future.

Healthy soils and healthy plants must have a balance of chemistry, physics, and biology.

Soil pH

The pH of the soil has been said to control the availability of the nutrients in the soil. That really isn't true. The pH of the soil is a *resulting* factor, not a *controlling* factor. It doesn't matter if the nutrients are provided by the application of a liquid or dry fertilizer or if the nutrients are supplied by the decomposition of soil minerals—their availability to the grass plant is controlled by biological activity within the soil. The pH of the soil will be around 6.5 when the soil is healthy, balanced, and rich in biological activity. Microorganisms affect the pH of the soil and are needed to convert plant nutrients from an unavailable form into a form the plant can use. These conversions are slower in both high- and low-pH soils.

The most common nutrient deficiency blamed on excessively high pH is iron deficiency. Many times there is enough iron in the soil, but it simply is not available to the plants. The condition called "chlorosis" is usually blamed on iron unavailability, and sometimes that is the case. What's more common is a deficiency of several trace minerals resulting from an imbalance of the physics, biology, and chemistry of the soil. Such soils are referred to as being "dead," but they are fixable with the Basic Organic Program (see www.dirtdoctor.com, Organic Advice, Guides, Basic Organic Gardening Program for complete details).

Salt Issues

In some soils, a salt buildup can create a serious problem for plants. The primary source of salt may be irrigation water, but the most common culprit is synthetic fertilizers. Turfgrasses vary in their ability to tolerate high soil salt levels. The first symptom of a salt problem is reduced growth. As salt levels increase, white salt deposits usually appear on the soil surface. A soil test can determine salt levels. While a few hundred parts per million (ppm) won't do any harm, most plants will be injured and even die if levels reach 1,000 ppm.

Salts can be leached out of the root zone, but the best long-term solution is the use of organic fertilizers and amendments.

Biology (Life of Soil)

The most important part of the soil is the soil life. While sand, silt, and clay are the mineral nonliving parts of the soil, organisms such as worms, nematodes, algae, fungi, and bacteria are just a few examples of the living parts of the soil. The most common soil organisms are bacteria and fungi. As many as 100 million bacteria per teaspoon may be present, although a few thousand is the usual population. Fungi populations are harder to estimate because they grow in threadlike strands and don't exist as individuals. Mycorrhizal fungi greatly expand the root system, increase nutrient availability, and protect plants against insect pests and diseases.

One of the most important functions of soil organisms is the conversion of the organic form of nitrogen to an inorganic form the plant can use. Bacteria convert organic nitrogen to the ammoniacal form of nitrogen (ammonium), which they use as their food supply. As long as there is a large source of carbon in the soil, such as organic matter, these bacteria will not use up all available nitrogen and plants will not suffer from nitrogen deficiency.

Healthy soil organism populations are critical to the production of healthy plants. For example, bacteria help keep fungi populations in check. Fungi are the number one cause of plant disease. Anything like excessively high or low pH, high salt levels, poor drainage, or excessive pesticides may serve to reduce the number of soil organisms, which in turn harms plant growth.

Diseases in grasses, as with all plants, are a matter of biological activity out of balance. Diseases are rare under an organic program because of the balance provided by the program. The most common fungal diseases can easily be controlled by stimulating the beneficial organisms in the soil. That can be done with compost, compost tea, cornmeal, molasses, and other natural materials. The microbes that we consider pathogens and disease organisms are actually beneficial in natural systems if they are there in their proper percentages and buffered by all the rest of the life in the soil. The reason the toxic chemical fungicides and other "cides" don't work is that they are indiscriminant. They kill *all* the life in the soil, good microbes and bad. When this semivacuum has been created, it doesn't last long. Life immediately starts to regrow. Unfortunately, the first living organisms to return are the microbes that, when out of balance, are the disease pathogens.

CHAPTER 2

Turfgrasses

Typical lawns have millions of individual grass plants growing in close proximity. Most other plants don't grow in such a crowded way. Grasses grow from a base "crown," so the tops of the leaves can be mowed regularly to a smooth, uniform, carpet-like appearance without killing or even greatly injuring the plant. Grass leaves, like all plant leaves, collect sunlight and are responsible for photosynthesis that feeds and makes the grass plant grow. In the process, the leaves take in carbon dioxide and exchange it for clean, pure oxygen that people and animals need for their growth. Lawns trap millions of tons of dust and other pollutants that are released each year into the atmosphere. Lawns can be as much as 30 degrees cooler than paved surfaces and 15–20 degrees cooler than bare soil in the summer. Grassy areas are also quieter than hard surface areas because of sound absorption.

Even though the aboveground benefits of turfgrasses are significant, what happens in the ground is even more important. A single grass plant can have miles of roots and even more miles of beneficial fungi when maintained with organic techniques. Grass roots, because of their density, also slow down irrigation and rain leaching and runoff so more moisture can be absorbed and kept in the soil. The result is a reduction of erosion and of the problems related to storm sewers becoming filled with silt and debris. Lawns can absorb rainfall far more efficiently than the bare soils of agricultural fields for example.

When grasses are maintained properly, leaf clippings are not caught but allowed to drop to the soil to rot and break down. As roots grow, portions slough off and die. Both of these sources of organic matter decompose through the help of beneficial microorganisms to form humus, feed plant roots, and build the health of the soil. This continuous cycle of growth and decomposition provides food for soil microorganisms, and in return, the microbes make major nutrients and trace minerals and enzymes available to the grass plants.

Beneficial microorganisms, including bacteria, fungi, actinomycetes, and protozoa, make the grass root zone their home. In a single pound of root-zone soil there will be hundreds of billions of microbes. One thousand square feet of healthy soil will have hundreds of pounds of microbes, microbe waste, and the dead bodies of microbes. These soil-building organisms require carbon as a source of energy. Carbon dioxide removed from the atmosphere by the grass plant becomes food for the microorganisms as plants decompose. The results are improved soils with available nutrients, increasing amounts of humus, and a reduction of carbon dioxide in the atmosphere.

As a return benefit to the grass and other plants, dead microorganisms provide nitrogen, phosphorus, potassium, and various trace minerals. This is fertilizing the natural way. The waste and dead bodies of microbes are the true natural fertilizers for plants.

Basic Turf Facts

Roots

The basic function of the root system is to provide water and nutrients the leaves need to manufacture carbohydrates that are the plants' food sources. The weakest turfgrasses have roots that are within the top few inches of the soil. The toughest and most drought-tolerant grasses have deep root systems and a greater ability to survive harsh weather of all kinds. Mowing practices, nutrient sources, soil types, and irrigation schedules and patterns can all influence the health and the size of the root systems of grasses.

The health of roots is based on more than just fertility. The proper chemistry from fertilizers is important, but for ideal growth and health, it must be balanced with the proper physics and biology. Biology is, of course, the life in the soil, and the physics relates to the tilth and aeration of the soil. Oxygen is a critical piece of the puzzle, but all three pieces must be in place for healthy growing conditions to exist. The organic program is the only way this natural balance can be achieved.

Crowns and Stems

Growth occurs in three places on the grass plant. The crown of the plant is found at the base of the plant near the soil surface. The leaf system is produced and grows vertically from this crown area. In some turfgrasses, the crown can be the source of laterally growing stems. When stems grow aboveground, they are called "stolons" or "runners." Stems growing underground are called "rhizomes." Some grasses, like Bermudagrass, have both, and some, like St. Augustine, have primarily one—in this case, aboveground stolons. On both stolons and rhizomes, joint structures called "nodes" develop. Nodes, like crowns, are growth sites and can produce whole new plants. Plants that do not produce seed reproduce by these lateral stems, or tillers, which are basically new small plants. The other site in the plant that is capable of growth is the tip end of each root.

Extensions of roots in healthy soil consist primarily of beneficial fungi called "mycorrhizae."

Leaves

Leaves are the food factories of the plant. They take the raw materials from the root system and turn them into the food material that the plant uses for growth. The process is called "photosynthesis."

The leaves may also be considered the plants' air-conditioning system. Water that enters through the root system that is not used in the food-manufacturing process passes out of the plant through tiny openings in the leaves called "stomata" in the form of water vapor. This process, which is called "transpiration," helps cool the plants.

Seasonal Growth Cycles

Turfgrasses have two basic seasonal growth periods of favorable weather. When the weather is not favorable for growth, the plant usually turns brown and enters a dormant period. During the dormant period, the plant is alive and living on its stored food reserves. Growth resumes when favorable weather returns.

The cool-season turfgrasses grow at their best during the cooler parts of the year, namely spring and fall. Their natural dormant period in the South is during the hot summer. Only tall fescue can be kept green during the heat of the summer in the South, but it requires high water use. It and other cool-season grasses are much easier to grow in more northern climates.

Warm-season turfgrasses have their best growth period during the hot summer months. During the cool fall months, leaf growth slows. During the fall, the leaf system is still manufacturing food, but instead of the plant using it for growth, it is being stored in the crown and underground parts. Turf must live on this stored food through its winter dormancy.

Optimum growth of the cool-season turfgrasses occurs when the temperature is in the 60–75-degree range. Growth in these plants begins to slow down when it gets below 40 degrees. The warm-season turfgrasses do best above 85 degrees. Growth stops at about 50 degrees.

Each time the temperature goes below freezing there is a danger that the warm-season turfgrass can be damaged or may even die. Some of the warm-season grasses can tolerate colder temperatures better than others. The amount of winterkill a lawn may experience depends on several factors: what kind of turfgrass, how quickly the temperature turns cold, how cold it gets, and how long it stays cold, and so on. The greatest chance for winterkill occurs in the spring when the lawn begins to green up and is hit by a late frost that damages and kills tender new tissue. Once this happens, the plant must dip into its storehouse of carbohydrate reserves to produce another leaf system when it is warm enough again. One late freeze may not be critical, but several could completely deplete the food reserves to a point of weakening the plants so that insects and diseases are encouraged and the plants might even die.

Reproduction

Turfgrass plants do not live more than a few years. Some only live one growing season. In most cases, as plants in the lawn die they are replaced automatically by plants produced by tillers, stolons, or rhizomes. These are the fastest-spreading grasses. Grasses, such as tall fescue, that produce tillers rather than runners are very slow spreaders. They are called "bunch" grasses. If these lawns thin out, it's usually necessary to reseed.

Most turfgrasses produce seed heads at some time or another, but the heads may or may not contain viable seed. Periodic seed-head production, especially in some Bermudagrass lawns, can be very unsightly, but only frequent mowing can offer any degree of control. Because some turfgrasses, mostly the Bermudagrass, do not produce viable seed, they are established either by sod or by stolons that are also called "sprigs." They are usually planted by hydromulching techniques.

Growth Requirements

All plants have the same basic requirements. They need a supply of water, a supply of nutrients, a certain quality and quantity of light, and the right temperature. Grasses, like all plants, make their own food (carbohydrates) through a process called photosynthesis. In this process, the plant uses carbon dioxide (CO_2), water (H_2O), and nutrients in the presence of light to make a sugar, with some oxygen released as a by-product. Only the plant cells containing the green pigment called chlorophyll can carry on photosynthesis. The food material may be used right away or stored as a reserve for the plant's use during stress periods, including summer or winter dormancy.

The process that turns food material into energy that the plant uses to grow is called "respiration." The difference between photosynthesis and respiration is shown in this table.

Photosynthesis	Respiration
Produces food	Turns food into energy
Energy is stored	Energy is used
Occurs in cells/chlorophyll	Occurs in all cells
Oxygen is released	Oxygen is used
Water is used	Water is produced
Carbon dioxide is used	Carbon dioxide is produced
Occurs in sunlight	Occurs anytime

The third basic process is called transpiration, which is the movement of water from the time it enters the roots until it exits as water vapor through small openings in the leaves called stomata. This upward stream of water carries nutrients to all upper parts of the plant. When water is changed from a liquid to a vapor in the plant, heat is released and the plant is cooled. In a sense, transpiration is the plant's air-conditioning system.

LIGHT

Light has three characteristics that affect plant growth: quantity, quality, and duration. Light quantity refers to the intensity of the sunlight. It is usually the highest at midday during the summer months. Light quality has to do with the type of exposure to sunlight—direct, filtered, or obscured/shaded—with direct sunlight being the best quality. Light duration refers to the length of time the plant is exposed to sunlight each day. This is called "photoperiod." It controls when a flower blooms and triggers the "hardening off" process just before the winter or summer dormant period begins.

The most common question I get is how to grow grass under trees. The truth is that both trees and grass want direct sunlight. Guess which one wins. Not only is there competition for light but also for water and nutrients. This problem gets worse as the tree roots get larger and more expansive. The solution is to remove trees—a move that's generally not the best—or to convert the ground area around trees to ground covers such as ivy, jasmines, and monkey grasses.

TEMPERATURE

Temperature has an effect on all plant growth processes, since plants have their ideal temperature ranges.

Turfgrass Selection

There are not that many different grass choices available for turf. The most popular lawn grass across the South is seeded Bermudagrass. Summer heat is not a problem, but the Bermudagrasses don't do well in the shade. Like other warm-season turfgrasses, they turn brown with the first frost in the fall. Some homeowners don't care for brown winter lawns. Bermudagrass is still the most popular grass of all because it is relatively easy to maintain as a green turf and is cheap to install. It grows only in full sun and can be a problem because of its aggressive habit of growing into planting beds while spreading by stolons and rhizomes. It looks fine growing mixed with St. Augustinegrass. Texturf-10 is a low-growing selection of common Bermudagrass. The step down to finer-textured Bermudagrass is Tifway 419, then Tifgreen 328 and dwarf tiffs, such as Tifdwarf, which are used on golf courses. Common Bermudagrass is less susceptible to diseases and insects than the dwarf hybrids or St. Augustine. I still use Bermuda some, but I prefer buffalograss in full-sun situations.

St. Augustine has the number two spot. It takes the heat as well as Bermudagrass and has the advantage of growing well in light to moderate shade. Its problem with cold temperatures limits its use to the southern states. St. Augustinegrass is a wider-bladed grass than Bermudagrass and can stand more shade—although it won't grow in heavy shade. It can freeze out in severe weather, even in the southernmost parts of the country. St. Augustine Decline (SAD) is a problem disease in the common variety, but not in the hybrid cultivar 'Raleigh'. Because St. Augustinegrass requires more water and care than Bermudagrass, it is farther down on my recommended list. It's a good choice for semishady areas in warm parts of the country, however.

There are some cool-season grasses that can be used in the South. Tall fescue can be used in shady areas if planted in the fall and lasts fairly well through the summer, and ryegrass can be planted as a fall "overseeding" to provide green lawns through the winter. Fescue is a heavy water user but is often used by golf course superintendents in shady rough areas where Bermuda and zoysias won't grow. This can also be done in the home landscape but usually needs to be replanted every fall. Fescue can be permanent in cooler climates.

Centipedegrass is more cold tolerant than St. Augustine and has some shade resistance. It grows best in acid soils, such as those of East Texas.

Buffalograss is popular for use in nonirrigated, low-use areas. Zoysia lawns are becoming more popular and offer a distinctive look for low-traffic areas. The only use for perennial ryegrass has been to overseed Bermudagrass lawns each fall for winter color. Buffalograss is the best choice for lawns in full sun. It has a soft, beautiful appearance and requires little water and even less fertilization. Some people have tried hard to convince us that the flowers of the male plants are ugly, but the wispy white flags that are often misidentified as seeds are actually quite attractive. If you are hung up on their appearance, female selections such as 'Prairie' or '609' are available. They are good but expensive. Whether you buy native or hybrid buffalograss, you'll be pleased with the low maintenance requirements. 'Stampede' is the only selection that has had some negative reviews.

Zoysia is an exotic-looking grass with thick, succulent dark-green foliage. The only problem with zoysia, other than that it won't grow in shade, is that it is so slow growing. I would never use it in an area that gets much foot traffic from people or pets. A dog or the mail carrier regularly walking the same path will kill it. For a beautiful grass to look at and not use too much, however, zoysia 'Meyer' is hard to beat. The other varieties, such as 'Emerald', aren't as good.

Cool-season grasses, those that grow in the cooler and colder parts of the country, include bentgrass, bluegrass, ryegrass, and fescue. These grasses are used as permanent grasses in cool or cold climates. Some are used for overseeding the warm-season grasses in the South, and they are also sometimes used in shady areas in warm climates. Cool-season grasses are of the bunch type rather than spreading like Bermuda and buffalo. All grasses are maintained in basically the same way, except that bunch grasses should be mowed higher than spreading grasses.

Bentgrass

Agrostis palustris (a-GROS-tis pah-LUS-tris)
Mowing Height: ⅛"–¼".
Mowing Frequency: 1–5 days.
Drought Tolerance: Moderate to low.
Shade Tolerance: Moderate.
Habit: A cool-season grass that is native to Asia and Europe. It prefers cool, humid weather, which makes it tough to grow in the southern summers. There are three types of bentgrass: 'Colonial', 'Creeping', and 'Velvet'. Spreads by creeping stolons.
Culture: Difficult to grow in hot and humid summers. Daily syringing, or light misting, is normally needed from June through September in the South. Light mistings of water are used to cool the turf by evaporation from the leaf surface. Watering, fertilization, mowing, and pest control must be closely managed to keep bentgrass green during the summer months.
Uses: Golf greens and specialty lawn areas. Primarily used on country club golf courses.
Problems: High maintenance due to heat stress. Doesn't like warm, humid nights. Sod webworms, cutworms, mole crickets, grubworms, dollar spot, brown patch, and other diseases.
Notes: Varieties available include 'Seaside', 'Pencross', 'Emerald', 'Penn Links', 'Cato', 'Crenshaw', 'SR1020', and 'Penneagle'.
Available as: Seed and solid sod.
Seeding rate: ½–1 pound of seed per 1,000 square feet. Use 50 pounds of mulch per 1,000 square feet. Water 2–4 times at least. Germination in 5–7 days.

Bermudagrass, Common

Cynodon dactylon (SIN-no-don DAC-ti-lon)
Mowing Height: 1"–2½".
Mowing Frequency: 3–7 days.
Drought Tolerance: Very good to excellent.
Shade Tolerance: Very low.
Habit: Warm-season grass that needs full sun. Has narrow leaf blades, spreads

by stolons and rhizomes, and is brown in winter. Still the most popular grass of all because it's relatively easy to maintain as a green turf and it's cheap to install. It only grows in full sun and can be a problem because of its aggressiveness in growing into planting beds while spreading by stolons and rhizomes. It looks fine growing mixed with St. Augustine. Finer-textured Bermudas are 419, then 328, and dwarf tiffs that are used on golf courses. Common Bermudagrass is less susceptible to diseases and insects than the dwarf hybrids or St. Augustine. Freeze damage is rarely a problem for common Bermudagrass.

Culture: Low-maintenance, aggressive grass. Grows in any soil. Does much better with ample water and food but is quite drought tolerant. Does not develop thatch.

Uses: Lawn grass, playing fields.

Problems: Some insects and diseases but none serious. Poor shade tolerance, grubs. It is a heavy feeder but can adapt to harsh conditions and has good wear tolerance.

Notes: Numerous seeded varieties with little difference are available. Texturf-10 is a low-growing selection of common Bermudagrass available in sod only. Mixing with St. Augustine and some weeds looks okay. Grass planting around new shrubs and trees will retard their growth. Texturf-10 is a dark-green variety, relatively free of seed stems and a good choice for athletic fields. Number one turfgrass of the South. Goes dormant (brown) during winter months. Native to Africa and other warm regions around the world.

Available as: Seed, sod, and sprigs.

Seeding Rate: 2 pounds per 1,000 square feet. It should be broadcast to the surface of loosened soil.

Bermudagrass, Tif (Tifgrass)

Cynodon dactylon cultivars (SIN-no-don DAC-ti-lon)
Mowing Height: ½"–¾" to 1".
Mowing Frequency: Weekly or more often on sports fields.
Drought Tolerance: Moderate to very good.
Shade Tolerance: Very low.
Habit: Warm-season grass for full sun. It is the hybrid form of common Bermudagrass. Narrower leaf blade and finer overall texture. Tifdwarf is the finest-textured, Tifgreen 328 is slightly larger, and Tifway 419 is the largest and is the best of the hybrids for residential use. Newest very small textured Bermudas are Champion, Tifeagle, and Mini Verde. These are becoming popular in the South on golf greens to replace bentgrass. Properly maintained, these warm-season grasses give high-quality putting surfaces and are far less trouble and less costly to maintain.

Culture: Higher maintenance than common Bermudagrass, since weeds and imperfections are much more visible.

Uses: Refined lawns and putting greens, also golf course tees and fairways. These grasses are sterile (no seeds) and must be planted solid or from stolons. Best used for high-maintenance home lawns, athletic fields, parks, and golf courses.

Problems: Some insects, such as grubs, and diseases but none serious. Needs to be mowed at least twice a week. Thatch can be a problem.

Notes: Tifway 419 and other varieties are not recommended for home lawns, as they require too much work. Takes traffic well. Not shade tolerant. Needs more water and fertilizer than common.

Available as: Sod or sprigs.

Stolon Rate: Stolons at 10–15 bushels per 1,000 square feet.

Bluegrass 'Reveille'

Poa arachnifera × *P. pratensis* (PO-ah ah-rack-NIF-er-ah × PO-ah pray-TEN-sis)
Mowing Height: 1½"–4".
Mowing Frequency: Weekly or as needed.
Drought Tolerance: Fair to good.
Shade Tolerance: Moderate to good.

Habit: 'Reveille' is a hybrid between Texas bluegrass (*Poa arachnifera*) and Kentucky bluegrass (*Poa pratensis*). Texas A&M University developed the cross in 1990 after twelve years of research. 'Reveille' will produce year-round green lawns for southern climates. 'Reveille' will grow in areas of the country where Kentucky bluegrass suffers from heat stress. Cold hardy and insect and disease resistant.

Culture: Easily established with sod all year except during the coldest parts of December and January. Hates wet feet. Don't water frequently. Cut to a height of 1½" to 2½". Avoid saline conditions. High heat tolerance. Stays green year-round with adequate summer moisture. Fair shade tolerance.

Uses: Best use would be partially shaded areas at homes where there are no dogs.

Problems: Susceptible to brown patch if overwatered. Also see the story below. This grass does not seem strong enough to recommend. It's too bad—I had high hopes.

Notes: Here's an interesting story about this grass. In the spring of 2002, I was contacted by a grass company about a new grass developed by Texas A&M, which was the one covered above. They asked if I would test this grass, and I was very interested. The concept sounded good—a cross of a native bluegrass and a cool-season turf bluegrass. The idea was that this hybrid would function as a turfgrass and grow in the shade out to a point where our native buffalograss would have enough sunlight to thrive. They brought it over and it was planted. It looked great, but I quickly learned that the organic program could not solve all the pest problems it was susceptible to.

For a week or so, this new grass looked terrific. I was excited, but all of a sudden curious brown spots started appearing in the turf. In a remarkably short time, the spots expanded, and within weeks the whole area was basically dead.

We figured it was some kind of disease pathogen or insect pest, but it became obvious that it was some serious kind of phytotoxicity because the grass turned brown and died quickly.

We finally figured out that it was indeed "fido"-toxicity—and that our dog was the culprit. Females are the worst about causing this grass damage, as they concentrate their urine in one place, but our little Tully possibly saved many homeowners some trouble and loss of money by exposing how weak this interesting new grass idea was.

Available as: Seed or sod.

Seeding Rate: 1 pound per 1,000 square feet.

Bluegrass, Kentucky

Poa pratensis (PO-ah pray-TEN-sis)

Mowing Height: 1½"–4".

Mowing Frequency: Weekly.

Drought Tolerance: Fair to good.

Shade Tolerance: Moderate to good.

Habit: Medium to fine leaf texture and a medium- to dark-green color when properly fertilized. It produces extensive underground stems (rhizomes), which give good sod-forming characteristics and excellent recuperative potential when compared to most other cool-season turfgrasses.

Culture: Seed germination and establishment is slower than for most other turfgrasses, requiring up to two weeks for emergence. It is cold tolerant, wear tolerant, and moderately heat and drought tolerant. Its optimum growth occurs during the spring and fall, and it becomes semidormant under prolonged periods of heat and drought. It usually recovers quickly from dormancy with cooler temperatures and adequate soil moisture. It performs best when grown in well-drained soils and open, sunny areas. It does not tolerate poorly drained soils or heavily shaded conditions, although a few varieties have improved shade tolerance.

Uses: Home lawns, institutional grounds, parks, and athletic fields.

Problems: Grubs. It is sensitive to low mowing heights and very susceptible to leaf-spot diseases as well as to dollar spot, stripe smut, necrotic ring spot, and summer patch.

Notes: This is a tough cool-season grass and performs well under an organic program.

Available as: Seed or solid sod.

Seeding Rate: 2–3 pounds per 1,000 square feet.

Buffalograss (Native)

Buchloe (or *Bouteloua* [boo-tuh-LOO-ah]) *dactyloides* (BUCK-low dac-ti-LOY-dees)

Mowing Height: 2" or not at all except for removal of old stubble in the spring.

Mowing Frequency: 7–14 days or 3–4 times per year for a more natural look.

Drought Tolerance: Excellent—by far the best.

Shade Tolerance: Low.

Habit: Warm-season low-growing grass with blue-green foliage and decorative flag-like flower heads that most people think are the seeds on the male plants. Best choice for southern lawns in full sun. The country's only native lawn grass has a soft, beautiful appearance and requires little water and even less fertilization. Some people have tried hard to convince us that the flowers of the male plants are unattractive. The wispy white flags that are often misidentified as seeds are actually quite attractive. If you are hung up on their appearance, sterile female choices such as 'Prairie' and '609' are available. They are excellent but expensive. Whether you buy native or hybrid buffalograss, you'll be pleased with the results.

Culture: Easy to grow in any soil except wet areas. Plant from seed in spring through September if irrigated. Grows better in heavier soils than in sandy soils.

Uses: Lawn grass, large natural areas, low-maintenance areas.

Problems: Slow to establish, but this is more an adjustment than a problem. Not shade tolerant.

Notes: Our only native lawn grass and the most drought-tolerant and low-maintenance grass of all. Fertilize only once with initial seeding. Do not water too much. Native from Texas to Minnesota and Montana.

Available as: Seed or sod. Spreads by stolons and seed.

Seeding Rate: 5 pounds per 1,000 square feet.

Centipedegrass

Eremochloa ophiuroides (er-ee-MOCK-lo-ah oh-fee-you-ROID-es)

Mowing Height: 1½"–3".

Mowing Frequency: 7–10 days.

Drought Tolerance: Moderate.

Shade Tolerance: Moderate.

Habit: Coarse-textured perennial grass that spreads by stolons. Stolons have a creeping growth habit with rather short upright stems that resemble a centipede. Propagated by seed or sod. Sometimes has a slightly yellow-green color. Naturally shallow rooted.

Culture: Grows in low-fertility conditions and has low maintenance requirements. Particularly well adapted to the sandy, acid soils where annual rainfall is in excess of 40 inches. Slightly more cold tolerant than St. Augustinegrass. Does not enter a true dormant state during winter months and is severely injured by intermittent cold and warm periods during spring. Water management is critical on heavy-textured soils during summer months. Not as drought tolerant as some people have been led to believe.

Uses: Home lawns, parks, golf course roughs, and utility turf. Ideally suited for roadside rights-of-way and other low-maintenance turf areas.

Problems: Does better in soils with a pH below 6.0. Few serious pest problems. Iron deficiencies may develop in the alkaline soils of the arid regions. Extended periods of 5°F or less can kill centipedegrass. Does not tolerate heavy traffic.

Notes: Has better cold tolerance than St. Augustine and nearly as good shade tolerance. Has poor wear tolerance. Native to China and southeast Asia. Introduced into the United States in 1916. Widely grown in the southeastern United States from South Carolina to Florida and westward along the Gulf Coast states to Texas.

Available as: Sod or seed.

Seeding Rate: 1–2 pounds per 1,000 square feet. One-third pound of seed should be uniformly mixed with about a gallon of fine sand and evenly distributed over 1,000 square feet. Seedbed should be kept moist, but not wet, for 14 to 21 days after planting.

Fescue, Tall

Festuca arundinacea (fess-TOO-cah ah-run-dah-NAY-see-ah)
Mowing Height: 2"–4".
Mowing Frequency: 5–7 days.
Drought Tolerance: Moderate to low.
Shade Tolerance: Moderate to good.
Habit: Deep-rooted cool-season perennial grass. Bunch-type grass. Used as a winter overseeding or as the primary grass in shady lawn areas. Used as a permanent grass in the cooler parts of the country. Has good shade tolerance.
Culture: Can tolerate fertility and responds well to regular feedings. Adapted to a wide range of soils but does best in fertile, well-drained soil. September is the ideal time for planting, but it can be planted through November. Grows to 3' when not mowed.
Uses: Lawn grass in shade, overseeding.

Problems: Low heat tolerance, leaf diseases such as fusarium blight, brown patch, and leaf spot. Armyworms, cutworms, and grubs. Must be mown all winter.

Notes: Best of the winter grasses for home use. Some people don't recommend it for overseeding, since it won't completely die out in the summer. Native to Europe. Can produce a year-round green turf if watered frequently during hot periods. Has good shade tolerance. 'Kentucky 31' and 'Alta' are the two oldest varieties in use today. To maintain a thick stand, mow down to 1" and broadcast 2–3 pounds of seed per 1,000 square feet every fall.

Available as: Seed.

Seeding Rate: 8–10 pounds per 1,000 square feet.

Paspalum

Paspalum vaginatum 'SeaIsle 1' (pass-PALE-um va-gee-NA-tum)

Mowing Height: ⅛"–2".

Mowing Frequency: 3–7 days.

Drought Tolerance: Good.

Shade Tolerance: Low.

Habit: Rich dark-green warm-season medium-textured grass that grows in a wide range of soils but does best in sandy soils. It has excellent resistance to drought and wear and is very salt tolerant.

Culture: Can tolerate most alternate water sources such as waste water, effluent, ocean water, gray water, and brackish water. Requires low levels of fertilization, irrigation, and pest management.

Uses: Excellent choice for fairways, tees, roughs, commercial landscaping, athletic fields, and reclamation projects.

Problems: Homeowners can use it but will need to mow more often and be aware of possible fungal problems.

Notes: 'SeaIsle 2000' has a blue-green cast and can be mowed even lower (⅛"). This is the grass used on the field at the Houston Astros' ballpark.

Available as: Solid sod.

Ryegrass, Annual

Lolium multiflorum (LO-lee-um mul-tee-FLOOR-um)

Mowing Height: 3"–4".

Mowing Frequency: 5–7 days.

Drought Tolerance: Moderate to low.

Shade Tolerance: Moderate to good.

Habit: Erect, robust cool-season bunch grass that reaches a height of 3 to 4 feet. Seedlings quickly establish a ground cover and are very competitive.

Culture: Tolerant of a wide range of soils and climates but is best adapted to valley and coastal areas with long seasons of cool, moist weather. Tolerates cold and can germinate in cooler sandy soils. Does better on heavier clay or silty soils with adequate drainage than in sandy soils. Tolerates extended wet periods and temporary flooding. Is moderately shade tolerant.

Uses: Winter cover crop, lawn, soil protection, and weed suppression. Used on poor soils. Heavy feeder and can be used to scavenge nitrogen from the soil during the fall and winter. Competes well with most weeds.

Problems: Competes with desired warm-season grasses in the spring if kept well watered.

Notes: Fall planting dates are from mid-September to mid-October.

Available as: Seed.

Seeding Rate: 5–7 pounds per 1,000 square feet.

Ryegrass, Perennial

Lolium perenne (LOW-lee-um per-REN-nee)

Mowing Height: 3"–4".

Mowing Frequency: 5–7 days.

Drought Tolerance: Moderate to low.

Shade Tolerance: Moderate to good.

Habit: Cool-season turfgrass native to Europe, temperate Asia, and North Africa. Resembles annual ryegrass but has more leaves in the lower part of the plant. The leaves are also thinner than annual ryegrass.

Culture: Tolerant of a wide range of soils and preferred as a winter overseeding grass, since it is easier to get rid of in the spring and therefore offers less competition to the summer grasses. Fertilize once during the growing season and mow weekly.

Uses: Lawn grass, livestock grazing forage.

Problems: Grubworms and various fungal diseases.

Notes: Best choice for winter overseeding.

Available as: Seed.

Seeding Rates: 5–7 pounds per 1,000 square feet.

St. Augustinegrass

Stenotaphrum secundatum (sten-no-TAY-frum say-coon-DAY-tum)

Mowing Height: 2"–4".

Mowing Frequency: 5–7 days.

Drought Tolerance: Moderate.

Shade Tolerance: Moderate to good.

Habit: Wide-bladed grass that spreads by stolons. It is the most shade tolerant of our warm-season grasses. 'Raleigh' is a hybrid resistant to St. Augustine Decline (SAD), and is more cold hardy than hybrids 'Seville' and 'Floratam'.

'Palmetto' is a dwarf variety and is more shade and cold tolerant. A wider-bladed grass than Bermuda, it can stand more shade, although it won't grow in heavy shade. It can freeze, as you know if you owned any in the winters of 1983 or 1989. St. Augustine Decline is a problem disease in the common St. Augustine but not a problem with the hybrid cultivar 'Raleigh'. St. Augustine requires more water and care than Bermuda and falls lower on the recommended list for that reason. It's a good choice for semishady areas. Needs four hours of full sun a day. 'Delmar' is an excellent shade- and cold-tolerant choice.

Culture: Any well-drained soil that is fairly fertile. Not as tough as Bermudagrass. Poor traffic tolerance. Plant only as solid sod. Reliable, hardy seed is currently not available. Spot sodding takes too long to cover.

Uses: Lawn grass for sun or part shade.

Problems: Chinch bugs, grubworms, brown patch, St. Augustine Decline (SAD), cold injury in the northern parts of the South and the country.

Notes: Native to Africa and the Gulf Coast.

Available as: Solid sod and plugs. No hardy seed available.

Zoysiagrass

Zoysia japonica 'Meyer' (ZOY-sha -PON-eh-kah)
Mowing Height: 1"–3".
Mowing Frequency: 5–15 days.
Drought Tolerance: Good.
Shade Tolerance: Moderate.

Habit: Warm-season succulent-looking grass for sun to part shade. Slow to spread by stolons and rhizomes. I would never use it in an area that gets much foot traffic from people or pets. A dog or the mail carrier walking the same path regularly will kill it. For a beautiful grass to look at and not use too much, zoysia is hard to beat.

Culture: Plant solid sod only, as it is too slow growing for any other planting techniques.

Uses: Lawn grass, small areas, Japanese gardens. Alternative to Bermudagrass or St. Augustine in some cases.

Problems: Slow growing—but that gives it its maintenance advantages. Thatch can be a problem if overfertilized.

Notes: Avoid using in high-traffic areas. Zoysia can be mowed less often than Bermudagrass and St. Augustinegrass, and it requires far less edging. Native to Japan and China. Only spreads about 6 inches per year.

There are three basic species of zoysiagrass: *Zoysia japonica*, *Z. matrella*, and *Z. tenuifolia*. They vary in cold hardiness and growth features. *Zoysia japonica*, Korean or Japanese lawn grass, was introduced to the United States in 1895.

It is more cold tolerant than the other species and has the coarsest texture. *Z. japonica* is the only zoysiagrass species that can be established from seed. Zoysiagrass 'Mcyer' is an improved strain of *Z. japonica* selected from plants grown from seed by the USDA in 1941 and named in honor of Frank N. Meyer, who made the first collection of zoysiagrass seed in Korea in 1905. 'Meyer' is slow to establish and must be propagated by sod or sprigs. Once established, it develops a very dense turf, demonstrates good cold tolerance, and grows well in light shade. It is well adapted to the transition zone where summers are too hot and humid for cool-season grasses and winters too cold for Bermudagrass. 'Belair' and 'El Toro' are new releases of *Z. japonica*. Both are coarser-textured but faster-spreading varieties than 'Meyer'.

Zoysia matrella was introduced into the United States in 1911 from Manila. It is more tropical, but can be grown as far north as Connecticut. *Z. matrella* grows well in moderate shade but better in full sun. Its leaf blades are narrow, sharply pointed, and wiry. In tropical climates, it stays green year-round, but in cooler climates, it is slow to establish.

Zoysia tenuifolia is the finest-textured, least winter hardy with fine, short, wiry leaf blades. It forms a dense, fluffy turf; is slow to spread; and is most often used as a ground cover.

'Emerald' zoysiagrass is a hybrid and combines the fine texture of *Z. tenuifolia* with the cold tolerance and faster rate of spread of *Z. japonica*. 'Emerald' is similar to *Z. matrella* in appearance and habit.

'Cavalier', 'Palisades', 'Royal', 'Zeon', and 'Zorro' are other available varieties. Zoysiagrasses can be established from sprigs or sod. *Zoysia japonica* is the only species that can be established from seed.

Available as: Sod or plugs but should only be planted as solid sod because of its slow growth. No seed available.

Seeding Rate for *Zoysia japonica*: 2 pounds per 1,000 square feet.

Quick Checklist for Grasses

Characteristic	Grass
Takes heat	All except tall fescue, perennial ryegrass, and Kentucky bluegrass
Grows in shade	St. Augustine, bluegrass, centipede, zoysia, Kentucky bluegrass
Year-round green color	Bluegrass, tall fescue
Takes traffic	Bermudagrass, buffalograss, paspalum
Low water requirement	Buffalograss, paspalum
High water requirement	Tall fescue, Kentucky bluegrass
Cold tolerant	Tall fescue, Texas bluegrass, Kentucky bluegrass, perennial ryegrass
Low height of cut	Hybrid Bermudagrass
Low fertility	Buffalograss
High fertility	Hybrid Bermudagrass
Winter color	Perennial ryegrass

CHAPTER 3

Lawn Establishment

Grass-planting techniques can be quite simple or very complicated and a huge waste of money. If you follow these simple tips, your lawn establishment will be enjoyable and affordable. When putting in a new lawn, remember one thing: If it's done right the first time, it should never have to be done again. By making careful plans and following these five basic steps, you can have a thick green carpet that you and your neighborhood will be proud of.

Soil Preparation

1. *Remove rocks and other debris from your yard.* Remove all objects that can cause problems later. For example, leftover construction debris, if buried, can cause drainage problems. Rocks or pieces of concrete near the surface can interfere with mowing. Buried organic material, such as pieces of lumber, will decay and lead to fairy rings or even cause an area of the lawn to sink. The debris most important to remove is that in the top 6 inches. Debris farther in the ground is not necessary to remove unless it blocks drainage in some way. Rocks within the soil are no problem because they help drainage.

2. *Kill the weeds.* Most new turf areas have weeds and maybe other unwanted grasses that need to be dealt with at the outset. Most annual weeds will be killed when the soil is tilled but not perennial weeds like Dallisgrass and Johnsongrass. It's very hard to control perennial weeds the first year of the new lawn. Therefore, the time to get rid of them is before the lawn is planted. The chemical folks recommend using herbicides such as those containing glyphosate, which is Roundup. All toxic chemical herbicides are dangerous, but this one is particularly bad because it has been marketed as completely safe and one that breaks down as soon as it hits the soil. The problem is that it not only stays around but is destructive to the beneficial life in the soil. The other problem is that it is used so ubiquitously. The truth is that it doesn't break down fast at all and is being found in the water supply. In addition, it is far more toxic than advertised. Research data on these facts can be found in the Library and Research section under the Organic Advice menu of dirtdoctor.com. My biggest concern is its damage to microbes in the soil. All toxic chemical herbicides are dangerous to

wildlife, pets, people, and the beneficial life in the soil, but the research is piling up that glyphosate (Roundup) is the worst of all.

Even after being killed, dead tissue should really be removed, so physical removal is actually the best approach. That way you are done once and for all. On the other hand, there are organic herbicides. They are made of citric acid, vinegar, fatty acids, and other nontoxic materials. Commercial products are available, but homemade mixtures work well also. See the appendix for home-made formulas. When applied properly, the organic weed killers work pretty well, but more than one spraying is sometimes needed.

3. *Apply fertilizer and soil amendments.* When planting grass seed, the addi-tion of organic material is beneficial, but strong fertilizer is unnecessary and can even hurt germination. Only on solid rock areas is the addition of native topsoil needed. Native soil is soil that is naturally present in your area. Imported foreign topsoil is a waste of money and can cause a perched (trapped) water table, the introduction of weeds, and other lawn problems. Mild organic fertilizers and amendments such as earthworm castings at 10 pounds per 1,000 square feet or humate at 10 pounds per 1,000 square feet (1 lb. per 100 sq. ft.) can be helpful.

Universities and extension agents in some parts of the country are advis-ing people to avoid products that contain phosphorus. That is very bad advice. Germinating grass seed, sprouting sprigs, and sod growing new roots all benefit from a good supply of phosphorus in the soil. It is a key nutrient necessary in grass establishment. Phosphorus moves downward very slowly into the soil when applied to the surface. It must be worked into the soil so that it will reach the grass plants' roots. Whatever fertilizer is chosen, grass growth will be more consistent and pest problems will be the lowest if the general health of the soil is increased with the addition of compost, humates, volcanic rock powders, and sugars such as dry molasses. All these materials stimulate biological activity and the production of organic matter (humus) in the soil. They all contain phos-phorus and will help release the phosphorus that's tied up in the soil but not available to the plant roots.

4. *Till the soil.* Seeds and sprigs should be slightly buried, and pieces of sod must be in contact with a loose soil surface. A loose, finely tilled soil will make this possible. In most cases, just till to a depth of 1 inch and rake the topsoil into a smooth grade. Deep rototilling is unnecessary and a waste of money unless the soil is heavily compacted.

5. *Rake the lawn area.* Rake the tilled soil and remove any rocks or debris that were brought to the surface when tilling. This raking should level the surface and smooth it to a degree, although there needs to be enough roughness to provide for good soil–seed contact. Spray compost tea or Garrett Juice over the area to be planted. Organic fertilizer should be applied to the soil at 10 pounds per 1,000 square feet prior to any of the three planting procedures.

Seeding, Sprigging, and Sodding

Selecting a method to use in establishing a lawn depends on the budget and the variety of the turfgrass to be planted. Sodding is the most expensive, followed by sprigging, plugging, and seeding.

Seeding

For warm-season grasses such as Bermudagrass or buffalograss, temperature is important when seeding a lawn. Night temperatures must be 65–70 degrees Fahrenheit for the seed to germinate and no lower than 40 degrees in the fall and winter for fescue, rye, and other cool-season grasses to be successful.

If you plant seed, the seedbed preparation is important. Lightly rake the seedbed before planting and after seeding to move the seed just under the soil surface. Next comes rolling. No matter what type of grass you use or how it is planted, the next-to-last step in installing a lawn is a light rolling that helps firm the soil and puts the seed or sprig in good contact with the soil. Rolling also helps eliminate any air pockets that might be present under the sod and lead to brown and dead spots in the newly laid sod.

For best results, treat the seed with Garrett Juice and mycorrhizal fungi prior to planting. Another option is to spray and drench the seeded area with the same materials after planting. After spreading the seed, thoroughly soak the ground and then lightly water as often as needed to keep the planted area moist until germination is complete. As the seed germinates and starts to grow, watch for bare spots. Reseed these bare areas immediately. Continue the light watering until the grass has solidly covered the area. At this time, begin the regular watering and maintenance program. For best results, do fertilize with a 100 percent organic fertilizer at 10 pounds per 1,000 square feet sometime before the first mowing.

Cool-season grasses such as fescue, ryegrass, bentgrass, and bluegrass should be planted for best results in late summer, such as September or October in USDA Hardiness Zones 7 and 8, although they can be planted anytime during the winter when the temperature is above 40 degrees. In all cases, the newly applied lawn seed should be watered regularly until the grass has grown to the point of covering the ground.

Fertilize turfgrasses three times a year the first few years of your organic program. Use an organic product at 20 pounds per 1,000 square feet in early spring (February–March), early summer (June), and fall (September–October). The rate and times of application can be reduced once healthy soil has been achieved.

Seeding rates are approximate, and the better job you do of preparing the soil, the better the chance that lower rates will be adequate.

Sprigging

Grass can be planted using seed or sprigs in the hydromulching process. A bushel of sprigs is equal to 1 square yard of shredded sod. A square yard of sod can be ground up and used to establish more than 20 square yards of a new lawn. Planting grass by hydromulching (a water, paper, seed, and fertilizer mix) should be done so that the seed is placed in direct contact with the soil. The seed should be broadcast on the bare soil first and then the hydromulch blown on top of the seed. One of the worst mistakes I see in grass planting is mixing the seed in the hydromulch slurry. This causes the seed to germinate in the mulch, which is suspended above the soil, so many of the seeds are lost from dehydration. Tifgrasses (Tifway 419, Tifgreen 328, and Tifdwarf) are dwarf forms of common Bermudagrass that must be planted by solid sodding or hydromulching sprigs with the same procedures as used for planting Bermudagrass seed. Tifgrasses are sterile hybrids and more expensive to maintain. They are okay for the golf courses, but I don't recommend these grasses for homeowners.

The rate usually used to sprig a lawn is from 5 to 7 bushels per 1,000 square feet.

SEED QUALITY

Here are some other factors to keep in mind when purchasing seed. On each box or bag of turfgrass seed is a label that contains some information that will help in evaluating the quality of that seed. The important things to look for are:

Purity: This is the percentage of pure seed in the container.

Germination: A percentage indicating how much of the seed in the bag will germinate. The term "Pure Live Seed," or PLS, is a number found by multiplying the purity (93.66%) by the germination (88%). The resulting 82 percent means that 82 percent of the material in the bag can establish grass plants if it receives proper care. The higher the PLS number, the better the seed.

Other Crop: This term is used to indicate the presence of any other turfgrass seed.

Inert: This is simply trash and should be as low as possible.

Weeds: This should also be low, and there should not be any noxious weeds.

Test Date: This should be fairly recent. Seed with an old test date may not be very good.

Certified Seed: This may be another label found on the seed container. The fact that it is certified has nothing at all to do with its quality in terms of purity or germination. The term *certified* means that an independent agency, such as a state university or the U.S. Department of Agriculture, has examined the fields and determined that it is indeed the particular variety of turfgrass indicated on the label. Buying certified seed is the only sure way to know that the variety of turfgrass in the container is what it says it is.

Sodding

Spot sodding is done by countersinking 4-by-4-inch squares into the ground flush with the existing grade and 12 to 14 inches apart after grading, then smoothing and leveling the soil. Organic fertilizer should be applied after planting at a rate of 20 pounds per 1,000 square feet. Regular maintenance and watering should be started at this time. This is not a planting procedure I highly recommend, however, because it is slow to cover an area and often results in an uneven, weedy lawn. It also leaves bare areas that are vulnerable to erosion and soil loss.

Solid sodding is the best means of grass planting. The squares of sod should be laid joint to joint after loosening the soil and establishing the proper final grade. Grading, leveling, and smoothing prior to planting is very important. Before planting, moisten the smoothed-out soil and then water the back side of the sod pieces before planting. The latter is a step that is rarely done but is very important to help avoid yellow and dead spots in the newly planted sod. The joints between the blocks of sod can be filled with compost to give an even more finished look. After planting, roll the sod to smooth it out and eliminate air pockets under the sod. Now it's time for the starter fertilizer. Use dry molasses or some organic blend that contains molasses at about 20 pounds per 1,000 square feet.

Laying and rolling solid sod

Early Lawn Care

Water lightly and often. Newly seeded or sprigged lawns should be kept moist, but not soaking wet and saturated. Frequent light waterings are necessary for good germination and establishment. This may mean watering two or three times a day for a while. If you've hydromulched or hydrosprigged, this many waterings a day may not be necessary. This regime should continue until the new young grass plants are visible. Then the frequency of watering should be reduced. After four to six weeks, the waterings should become fairly infrequent and the new lawn should be treated the same as an established one.

If you plant sod, it should be soaked completely each time it's watered and should be watered again when it begins to dry out. In about two weeks, the roots should be developed enough that you should be able to water at fairly infrequent intervals as with an established lawn.

Mowing. Generally, the more often a new lawn is mowed, the faster it will spread and form a thick, dense turf that resists weed invasion. Keep the mower blades sharp so the cuts are smooth and don't encourage pathogens.

Continue weed control. Weed control should be done by mechanical means (hoes, weed poppers, etc.), hand removal, or spot-spraying of an organic herbicide such as vinegar. Mowing usually controls most annual weeds, and they are the most common weed issues early on.

Problems Establishing Grass

Although the grass establishment process is usually fairly easy, problems can arise. Here are a few of the most common ones to watch for:

1. *Not enough water.* This is common with lawns seeded during the hot, dry summer. Newly planted grass must be kept moist and not be allowed to dry out in the first few weeks.

2. *Too much water.* This usually happens during rainier times of the year and may cause diseases to develop. Common Bermudagrass that is overwatered turns a purple or reddish-purple and the soil may erode. Other grasses have similar symptoms. Simply reduce watering to cure either problem.

3. *Overfertilized.* New turf can be damaged badly by synthetic fertilizers because they are salts and can burn quickly. Even organic fertilizers can damage newly planted grass if grossly overused. They usually don't kill the grass but can damage and slow down the establishment.

4. *Overwatered and overfertilized.* These lawns, if they live at all, develop a very shallow root system and may not make it through the first winter.

5. *Perennial weeds.* These weeds can give the new grass plants some serious competition. This is a direct result of not taking measures to control weeds before planting the grass.

CHAPTER 4

Maintaining the Lawn

Once you've got the soil properly improved, and you've planted the right grass, how do you keep a lawn healthy and green? There are eight major components to lawn maintenance: mowing, watering, fertilizing, controlling weeds, controlling pests, controlling diseases, aerating, and dethatching.

Mowing and Edging

People like neatly mowed and edged grass. The look is nice, and the smell of freshly mowed grass is very pleasant to most people. It's as simple as that as to why it is so important. When considering the effects that mowing can have, remember that grass plants are designed by nature to grow and mature to a much taller height than that at which they are maintained in a lawn. Mowing, in a sense, is not normal because it tends to upset the natural growth patterns of the plant.

Mowing is required for aesthetics and certain horticultural needs. Mowing doesn't hurt grass plants; in fact, it encourages the grass plants to grow and expand. When the blades are cut off, plants have to grow new leaves to absorb sunlight. This helps build a thicker, heavier lawn, which is more resistant to weeds and disease.

It's best to mow frequently during the growing season. The rule of thumb is to never cut off more than a third of the grass plant at once. One common mowing mistake is cutting the grass too short. It's best to keep cool-season grasses at about 3 inches high or taller, and most warm-season grasses do well at about 1½ to 2½ inches high. The shade provided by the leaves will help cool the soil, and greater leaf surface aids photosynthesis. Bermudagrass is the one grass that likes to be mowed really low.

When mowing, vary the pattern to avoid creating ruts in the turf caused by the wheels rolling in the same place every time. Dull mower blades is another issue. Avoid this problem by sharpening mower blades at least three times a year to ensure a healthy, clean cut. Catching the clippings is another bad idea. Clippings should always be left on the turf. Nothing but good things result from this policy.

> The single most important change I recommend to homeowners in turf management is to stop catching the clippings. They should be mowed, mulched, and left on the lawn. I'd get rid of the grass catchers.

To establish a quality lawn, it might be helpful to understand a little bit about how the turfgrass plant reacts to mowing. The first effect of mowing is the reduction of the plant's leaf surface area. Leaves manufacture and supply the plant with carbohydrates, which is the plant's food. During the active growing months (spring and fall for the cool-season grasses and summer for warm-season grasses), carbohydrate production is high and the plant is able to store food reserves. During periods of stress or dormancy, the plant must draw on these reserves to survive.

When part of the grass plant's leaf system is removed by mowing, the plant reacts by using high amounts of carbohydrates to replace the leaves that were cut off. Since the leaf system has priority over the other plant parts for carbohydrates, root and lateral stem growth is greatly reduced. Only when the leaves are replaced does root and stem growth renew. The greater the amount of leaf surface that is cut off at each mowing, the longer the root and stem growth is reduced.

Research through the years has established the best mowing height for each of the grasses and has also found that when no more than one-third of the leaf system is removed at one cutting, the negative effects on the root and stem

Recommended Mowing Heights

Turfgrass	Best Mowing Height	Mow When Lawn Is
Common Bermudagrass	1½ inches	2¼ inches
Hybrid Bermudagrass	1 inch	1½ inches
Kentucky Bluegrass	2 inches	3 inches
Texas Bluegrass	2 inches	3½ inches
Buffalograss	3 inches	4½ inches
Centipedegrass	2 inches	3 inches
Perennial Ryegrass	2 inches	3 inches
St. Augustinegrass	2 inches	3 inches
Tall Fescue	2 inches	3 inches
Zoysiagrass	1½ inches	2¼ inches

growth are minimal. For example, the ideal cutting height for a common Bermudagrass lawn is 1½ inches. Ideally it should not be allowed to get any higher than about 2¼ inches. A St. Augustine lawn should be cut at 2 to 2½ inches, when it gets to be 3 to 3½ inches high.

Cutting height has a direct effect on root size. The grass plant, just like all other plants, develops a balance between its aboveground parts and its root system. A certain size of root system is needed to support a certain volume of top growth and vice versa. If either the top part or the root system is reduced, the plant will react by reducing the other. When the turfgrass is mowed, its top growth is obviously reduced. With less foliage, plants no longer need the same size root system and reduce it to achieve balance. The more top growth that is removed (i.e., the lower the cutting height), the shallower the root system may become, which can seriously reduce the plant's ability to withstand stresses, such as that caused by drought. On the other hand, some grasses such as Bermudagrass respond to low cutting by increasing lateral growth and actually becoming thicker.

Insulation is another important function of the leaf system. Growing points, or crowns, of most turfgrass plants are at or near the surface of the soil, and they conduct chemical activities that control the growth processes. These growing points are temperature sensitive. The upper optimum temperature range for cool-season turfgrasses is about 75 degrees and about 85 degrees for warm-season turfgrasses. When the temperature at the growing point goes above these temperatures, the growth process slows down. If the temperature at the growing point gets too high for a long enough period, especially with cool-season grasses, the plant goes into what is called summer dormancy.

Foliage of the grass plants insulates the growing points from high temperatures. When mowing reduces foliage surface area, insulation protection available for the growing point is reduced. Thus, mowing a cool-season grass such as tall fescue too low will make it more susceptible to high temperature injury.

Most turfgrasses are subjected to some degree of wear. Golf course putting greens and athletic fields and play areas in home lawns generally receive the highest wear. When the leaf surface is reduced, the overall durability of the turf is reduced. Turf cut at low heights is subject to high-wear damage and tends to thin out gradually. Compaction of the soil in the high-use areas is directly related to the damage of the turf. Physical compaction reduces the oxygen in the roots and adversely affects the beneficial life in the soil. The end result is stressed, poor-performing turf. The continued use of high-nitrogen synthetic fertilizers causes the same problem.

Mowing practices can have an effect on the incidence of disease. When grasses are weaker and stressed because of being cut too low, the opportunistic pathogens and insects are most likely to attack.

If high rates of nitrogen are applied to a lawn, the frequency of mowing must be increased. This is especially true when the nitrogen is supplied in a soluble form. That's one of the main reasons to avoid synthetic fertilizers. If because of high growth rates the lawn has to be mowed too frequently, you should consider adjusting both the nitrogen rate and its source. The simple answer is to switch to organic products. The slower-releasing nitrogen materials and organic nitrogen sources do not tend to produce the lush growth in big spikes and will allow a longer period between mowings.

In most situations, grass clippings should not be removed during mowing. Removal may be required when the clippings interfere with a specific use of the turf. This applies to golf course putting greens, bowling greens, or croquet courts, or when, because of rain or missed mowings, the clippings are too heavy and tend to look bad or even smother the turf. Generally, the shorter the clippings, the better they tend to fall deep into the turf and the more rapid their decomposition. For most projects, grass clippings provide nutrients and do not contribute to thatch, so there is no need to bag them if a reasonable mowing program is followed.

Proper selection of height of cut, proper mowing frequency, the use of a mower with a sharp blade, and the development of a reasonable growth rate can all have a profound effect on the health and vigor of any turfgrass system.

Lawn Mower Selection

Price, as with most things we buy, seems to have a great influence on our selection of a lawn mower. And while there is no question about the importance of price, other considerations should also play a part in the selection of a lawn mower.

In general, the upper cutting height limit for a reel-type mower is about 2 inches. The lower cutting height limit for a rotary-type mower is about 1 inch. The variety of turfgrass in the lawn should be considered in the selection of the mower type.

Most turfgrass experts suggest that a reel-type mower has a superior cutting action to that of a rotary. The scissor-like cutting action of the reel type tends to produce a cleaner cut on the leaf blade. If a rotary mower's blade is kept sharp, it also will produce a clean cut. If you select a rotary mower, it might be wise to pick up an extra blade so that you can replace the dull blade with a sharp one every month or so. This gives you a month to get the blade sharpened before it is due to go back on the mower.

Some lawn mowers are advertised and sold specifically as mulching mowers. They will cut up the leaf blades and other lawn debris into smaller pieces that will decompose faster, but if the lawn is cut with any mower so that no more than a third of the leaf blade is removed at any one mowing, the resulting clippings are usually small enough that they will decompose fairly rapidly and not

Manual reel-type mower

contribute to any thatch. If you tend to let your grass get too long between mowings, a mulching mower will definitely be a benefit. It's better for the lawn to be mowed more frequently than to let it get too high and have to rely on the mulching action of a mower. When using organic fertilizers, it is rarely necessary to mow more than once a week.

You should determine if the engine of the gas power mower you are considering is either two or four cycle. A two-cycle engine burns a gas-oil mixture, while a four-cycle engine uses straight gasoline. A four-cycle engine requires an oil change at certain intervals, but a two-cycle does not. Four-cycle engines do not produce harmful air pollution as much as the two-cycle engine produces. There are several other mower options these days that are worth considering.

Manual Reel-Type Mowers

These old-timey, historic throwback mowers have become popular again from several standpoints. They are quiet and don't create the sound pollution of gas-powered machines, they don't pollute the air, and they save money. They also provide some good exercise.

Electric Mowers

Yes, electric mowers are still available. The noise pollution is less when using these, and exhaust pollution is nonexistent. These are pretty good mowers except for the fact that the cord is a pain in the neck and can be dangerous.

Lithium battery–powered mower by Stihl

On the other hand, there is something new and exciting on the market. The Stihl company has introduced a complete line of lithium battery–powered tools, including chainsaws, hedge trimmers, and blowers but also a terrific edger and two mowers. These tools are of very high quality and are all I use at home and at our experimental gardens. The key is the long-lasting, easy-to-charge battery that is interchangeable in all the pieces of equipment. I have used Stihl chainsaws, sprayers, and hand pruners for years, but these new battery-powered tools are state of the art, and I highly recommend them.

Riding Mowers and Lawn Tractors

These machines are used a lot for large sites and on sites of any size by people who like expensive toys. They are great if you have big areas of grass to mow. They are heavy and bulky and not practical for most homeowners with small- to average-sized lawns. They are not even practical for some businesses, as you'll notice in one of the photographs.

Robot Mowers

These strange-looking little mowers are questionably effective and probably not worth the money, but they do provide interest for the curious neighbors and good coffee-table subject matter.

Propane Mowers

These machines are becoming more and more available, and kits are available for converting gasoline-powered machines to this alternative fuel. They are less noisy and less polluting.

Some other considerations in selecting a mower are ease of mowing-height adjustment, ease of blade removal and replacement (rotary), ease of oil changing if it is a four-cycle engine, and the location of the controls. Also, you might consider whom you are buying the mower from—you may need some service later on and you want to be sure it can be provided. If a reel-type mower is selected, the number of blades on the reel and the intended height of cut should be considered.

Edging and Trimming

Edge the turf along walks and curbs weekly. Use monofilament trimmers or hand trimmers along steel edging, curbs, and other hard surfaces but never around trees or shrubs. A lot of damage has been done by these devices in the name of convenience. Edging around trees and shrubs should be done with vinegar or other organic herbicide sprays. The vinegar spray kills the grass and weeds and does not hurt the woody plant tissue at all.

Line trimmers are good tools, but they need to be used with some common sense. For example, do not scalp grass while using line trimmers. Edging is needed for aesthetics just to keep things tidy. Edge around turf irrigation heads where tall grass is disrupting the irrigation coverage. Edgers are not for the purpose of eliminating other more appropriate tools for specific jobs.

Scalping

Each spring, many homeowners go through the curious process of setting their mowers on the lowest setting and removing the dead grass from their lawns. This process has been called "scalping" and, more incorrectly, "dethatching."

Spraying vinegar herbicide around trees helps avoid damage to trunks from weed whackers and mowers. Photo by Doreen Kozlowski.

It not only removes the dead stubble but also exposes bare soil. Both of these things are bad. Thatch is the name of this layer of organic material that under certain unhealthy conditions may develop between the base, or crown, or the plant and the soil surface.

Some think that this scalping procedure helps the grass green up earlier in the spring. The reason scalped lawns "turn" green earlier is that the physical removal of all the brown leaf material allows more of the green leaves to be visible.

Scalping turf in the spring is not a part of any professional turf management program. Athletic fields, golf courses, and similar areas are maintained without scalping. Scalping is a dirty, unpleasant job, and in an average-sized city this practice can generate hundreds and thousands of bags of grass material. Many of these bags find their way to area landfills where space is already at a premium. Many cities must pay overtime in the spring just to deal with this tremendous volume of dead grass, and, of course, the irony of the situation is that this is all unnecessary. Scalping is not necessary to produce a good-quality lawn. In fact, it is a complete waste of time and money. Proper mowing techniques, the timely use of the right fertilizer, and the timely application of water work together to produce a quality lawn.

Grass clippings aren't the problem. It's my strong opinion that grass clippings should never be caught when mowing home lawns and most commercial landscapes. An easy way for this bad practice to be eliminated is for cities to stop picking up grass clippings or other organic materials such as leaves. If home-owners have to manage the organic matter on their properties, their turf and landscaping will be better and the cities will save a lot of money. The pickup and storage of this organic material is anti-environmental and wastes a lot of city and taxpayer money.

Chemical Mowing with Growth Regulators

Chemicals that affect growth rates of grasses have become popular, especially on golf courses. The concept is that if the grass grows slower, not as many mowings are needed. Primo is one of the most commercially available products. The only problem is that chemicals that affect plant growth almost always have a negative influence on the plants and often on the soil as well. One of the issues with the growth regulators is that they produce lateral rather than vertical growth. That's a bad thing, especially in sports turf, because it causes severe grain in the grass, meaning that the grasses grow laterally in one direction, which is bad for golf shots and bad for running and turning on sports fields.

Watering the Lawn

Watering Frequency

It's impossible to give specific instructions on how often and how much to water. There are too many variables: soil, drainage, weather, climate, sunlight, etc. The general rule is to water heavily and deeply, when the lawn really needs it, rather than watering lightly more frequently. And then skip as much time as possible before watering again. Watering lightly causes shallow roots, stressed grass, and wasted water. Some advisers recommend watering enough to get the moisture 6 to 8 inches deep, putting out about an inch of water with each irrigation, but that's not going to work in many cases. Each site's irrigation requirements will be different, and the schedule should be customized.

Water as the grass starts to dry out and the color fades somewhat. If grass doesn't spring back quickly after you step on it, it needs water. The best time to water is in the early morning, as the water won't evaporate as easily as in the afternoon. On the other hand, it rains at all times of the day, and that seems to work well.

Watering is a critical issue and getting more serious every year. It is one of the most basic practices in maintaining a home landscape and lawn. All sites need periodic watering, but the requirements can vary tremendously. Like most of our landscape plants, the turfgrasses, with the possible exception of buffalo-grass and maybe common Bermudagrass, may not survive severe dry summers without the judicious application of water.

In many parts of the country, water availability is already very limited, but it's a serious component of good site management anywhere. In other areas, water quality may be a problem. Highly acid, highly alkaline, or salty water can cause serious problems and make plant growth very difficult. In areas of low water availability and low water quality, it is even more critical that the lawn be watered correctly. The organic program can help solve all these issues.

Watering the Correct Amount

Just as the lack of water has a negative effect on plants, so does too much water. The root system of a plant must take in oxygen and give off carbon dioxide to live. When water is applied too frequently, the soil becomes saturated and anaerobic. The movement of oxygen into the soil and carbon dioxide out of the soil is reduced or shut off. This results in a condition in the plant termed "wet wilt," which, if not corrected, causes severe plant stress and leads to other problems, including death. The bottom line is that if roots can't breathe, they die.

Soil type has a great influence on water management. Many soils are high in the type of clay that tends to shrink when dried. It is not uncommon to see large cracks develop in lawns during the dry summer. While the development of these cracks usually does not cause serious damage to turfgrass, the cracks certainly can pose a safety hazard for those using the lawn as a play area. Also, if a house is built on these soils and the soil is allowed to dry to the point of cracking, the foundation of the house may also crack. Watering the landscaping around the house in a reasonable way and using the organic program are the answers to this possible problem.

The amount of water needed varies greatly among the turfgrasses, and consideration of this fact when establishing a lawn may significantly reduce the need for irrigation during the summer. Turfgrasses that require low water should be considered in areas of low water quality or low water availability.

Watering New Lawns

Newly seeded or sprigged lawns should be watered lightly at frequent intervals for best results. The key is that the seed, sprigs, and even solid sod, especially during the summer, must be kept moist but not saturated during this initial growth period. An application of water might be necessary as many as four or five times on hot, windy days. The first ten to fourteen days is especially critical. If young plants are allowed to dry out, they will die. After about two weeks, the development of root systems should be well under way, and the watering frequency should be reduced slowly. About one month after seeding or sprigging, the new lawn should be treated as an established lawn. Purple or red seedlings of some grasses, such as Bermudagrass, may be a symptom of overwatering. If this occurs, reduce watering and the plants usually recover.

Newly sodded lawns should be watered much like established lawns, except more frequently. After the sod is applied, it should be soaked with enough water so that the soil under the sod is wet to a depth of 2 to 3 inches. Each time the sod begins to dry out, it should be resoaked. Roots develop fairly rapidly, and within two weeks or so, it should be ready to be treated like an established lawn. One of the best tips for planting new sod is to water the back side (soil side) of the new turf pieces before they are put in place. Toss the sod pieces on the ground upside down and water with a hose prior to setting the sod in place. If this procedure is done—and it's not hard—no yellow spots will show up at all. Another good tip is to roll the sod after planting. This isn't so much for leveling purposes as it is to eliminate the air pockets under the sod. Again, no yellow spots will be the result.

Watering Established Lawns

Ideally, a lawn, no matter what the grass type, should be watered just before it begins to wilt. Most grasses take on a dull purplish cast and the leaf blades begin to fold or roll in. Grass under drought stress also shows evidence of tracks after someone walks across the lawn. These are the first signs of wilt. With careful observation, it is not too hard to determine just how many days a lawn can go between waterings. Common Bermudagrass lawns should be able to go five to seven days or even longer between waterings without loss of quality. St. Augustine requires a shorter time between waterings, but buffalograss can go for a long time. Buffalograss is so drought tolerant that irrigation can be completely stopped without injuring the grass. It will go dormant and turn a golden brown color but will green up quickly with rain or irrigation.

Early morning is considered the best time to water. The wind is usually calmer and the temperature is lower, so less water is lost to evaporation. The quicker the grass plants dry off after irrigation, the better. A high percentage of water is lost to evaporation when turf is watered during the heat of the day. On the other hand, remember that it rains at all times of the day. Therefore, no matter what time of day it is, if the turf is thirsty, water it.

How Much Water

When a lawn needs to be watered, enough water should be applied so that the soil is wet to a depth of about 4 to 6 inches. The type of soil has a great deal to do with how much water is needed to wet soil to the desired depth. It should take about ½ inch of water to achieve the desired wetting depth if the soil is high in sand, and about ¾ inch of water if the soil is a loam. For soils high in clay, an inch of water usually is necessary to wet the soil to the desired depth.

If the water application rates are too light or too frequent, the lawn may tend to become weak and shallow rooted, which makes it more susceptible to stress injury along with insect pests and diseases.

How to Water

The following technique will allow you to find out how much water your sprinkler or sprinkler system puts out and to check its distribution pattern at the same time.

1. Determine the rate at which your sprinkler applies water to the lawn.
   a. Set out three to five empty cans in a straight line going away from the sprinkler. Set the last can near the edge of the sprinkler's coverage.
   b. Run the sprinkler for a set period of time, such as one-half hour.
   c. Measure the amount of water in each can. This tells you how much water is put out in 30 minutes.
2. Run sprinkler or sprinkler system long enough to apply at least 1 inch of water or until runoff occurs.
   a. Stop sprinkler and note running time.
   b. Allow water to soak in for half an hour or longer.
   c. If runoff occurs, increase work to improve soil health.

> Water long enough for deep penetration and then skip as much time as possible before watering again. Watering often with short cycles is bad practice.

Other Factors

Soil type: Water penetrates a sandy soil much faster than a clay soil, so lawns grown on sandy soils will require more frequent watering than those grown on soils that are high in clay. Because water moves fairly slowly into a clay soil, the rate at which water is applied to this type of lawn should be done as slowly as possible.

Slope: Lawns with moderate to steep slopes present a particular problem. It is very easy for water to run down the slope without penetrating the soil. Water must be applied at very slow rates from sprinklers near the top of the slope. Sprinklers on the slope or near the bottom of the slope may prove ineffective. Again, healthy organic soils will accept the water much more efficiently, even on slopes.

Watering Equipment

Drip irrigation is one way to water, but I'm not a fan. It is probably necessary in some agricultural situations, but I really don't trust drip systems for several reasons. They are always in the way and easy to tear up because they are partially or completely hidden. Rodents eat holes in the lines, and the material wears out and rots.

The reason all that's important is that when drip irrigation lines crack, or spring a leak in any way, the water floods some areas and leaves other areas dry. Even if there are no failures and leaks, water naturally seeks the path of least resistance and produces uneven moisture in the soil. Since you can't see where the water is going with a drip system, roots can rot or dry out completely and die before you realize there is a problem.

What's a better way to go? Sprinkle the plants from above. The water is visible, you can monitor easier, and there is much less chance of disaster. Does water on the foliage cause disease problems? Well, it rains at night and that doesn't seem to be a big problem.

The faster the lawn grows, the more water it requires. The synthetic fertilizer proponents recommend slow-release fertilizers that contain materials such as sulfur-coated urea or urea formaldehyde as nitrogen sources. Their reasoning is that these fertilizers do not tend to produce growth rates as high as do the synthetic fertilizers high in soluble nitrogen. All this is a feeble attempt to try to come up with synthetic fertilizers that will behave a little bit like organic fertilizers. Why not just use organic fertilizers?

The use of an aerator or coring device will aid in increasing movement of water into the soil. A surfactant, or wetting agent, also may aid the movement of water into high-clay soils. The truth is, organic fertilizers and amendments do all that and more.

All the water in the world can't help a lawn if it is not applied efficiently. A great array of both aboveground and belowground irrigation equipment is available for home lawn use. In making a choice, there are a number of things to consider.

Application Pattern: It doesn't make too much sense to use a portable sprinkler that produces a square or rectangular pattern when the lawn has a basically round shape. In-ground systems are designed to fit the shape of the lawn. If aboveground sprinklers are used, care must be taken in their selection to make sure they provide an even pattern of water, regardless of whether it has a round or square shape. Typically, these sprinklers must be moved around the lawn, which may have an effect on just how evenly the whole lawn gets watered. Generally, the chances are better of getting a good, even application of water on the lawn when a well-designed in-ground sprinkler system is used—unless the operator of the aboveground system has taken great care in the selection of the hose and sprinkler and in its operation.

Droplet Size: Regardless of the type of system selected, the size of water droplet the sprinkler head produces is important. The finer the droplet size, the easier it is for the designed pattern of that sprinkler head to become distorted by wind. In many areas, such as my hometown of Dallas, it may be a rare day when the wind doesn't blow. Large droplets are not as easily distorted by the wind as small ones. Another problem associated with a system that produces fine water droplets is the fact that small droplets are more subject to evaporation than large droplets.

Application Rate: It is very important to find out just how long it takes the sprinkler or sprinkler system to apply a certain amount of water. With this information, you'll know how long to run the system or how often the hose-end sprinkler needs to be moved.

Operation Ease: An in-ground system with an automatic controller is by far the easiest to use. Since the best time to water is in the early morning, that fact alone might help one select an automatic system. However, I think it is important to keep the automatic settings of control clocks off. Too often, people forget to turn them off when it rains. They also forget to cut back the frequency and volume of water when the weather turns cool and the days get shorter. I strongly advise leaving irrigation timers on manual settings so that the only time the system waters is when you push the button to allow it to cycle through the sections that water different parts of the landscape. It's also an important way to save water by preventing the system from running when water isn't needed.

There are highly technical weather stations now available that monitor the wind, the temperature, and the humidity and moisture in the soil to automatically control the frequency and volume of water being applied. They are marketed as a scientific way to control irrigation and save water. I have heard mixed reports on the systems, and they are very expensive. The less costly in-ground moisture systems that can help contractors and homeowners decide when to water seem to be better investments.

How to Buy a System: There are many companies selling and installing irrigation systems. The best way to choose a contractor to install your system is to ask for and talk to references. Your irrigation system will only be as good as the company that installs it.

Watering Summary
- Apply enough water to wet the soil to a depth of 4 to 6 inches.
- Avoid frequent light applications of water.
- Water in the early daylight hours.
- Select a turfgrass that has a low water requirement.
- Avoid using high rates of soluble nitrogen fertilizers. They tend to promote high growth rates that increase the water requirements of the plant.
- Avoid drip and leaky-pipe watering systems.
- Use the manual versus the automatic setting on the sprinkler system controller.

Fertilizing the Lawn the Chemical Way

Lawns that are underfertilized are often thin and have poor color, whereas lawns that are overfertilized, especially with high-nitrogen soluble fertilizer, will develop excessive thatch and be prone to insect and disease damage. The key to quality fertilizers is to select products that contain carbon and work efficiently to stimulate biological activity in the soil.

Required Nutrients

All plants, including grasses, require major nutrients as well as trace minerals for proper growth. The soil, in most cases, is a vast reservoir of these plant nutrients, but soils vary in the amount of nutrients they contain and in their ability to release those nutrients to plants. When a plant requires more of a nutrient than the soil can supply, or requires a nutrient not present in the soil, then a fertilizer must be used. Soil tests can be helpful, but some soil tests only measure the nutrients that are present in the soil. They give no information on what nutrients are *available* to the plants. One testing lab, in Edinburg, Texas, does things a little differently. They use a carbon dioxide extraction method and also offer organic recommendations. This is the only testing lab I currently recommend. They also offer tissue sample testing, water testing, compost testing, and testing for contaminants. All this can be quite helpful in turfgrass management.

Of all the nutrients required by the turfgrass plant, three—nitrogen (N), phosphorus (P), and potassium (K)—are often not readily available in the soil in high enough quantities for good growth and must be added periodically in fertilizer form. This has more to do with availability of nutrients to the plants than their physical volume. In some special situations, such as when soils are highly acidic or alkaline, other nutrients such as iron or magnesium may need to be added until the biology has been increased and the tied-up nutrients start to become available. The only way to know for sure is to get a proper soil test done. Texas Plant and Soil Lab (TPSL) is one testing lab using carbon dioxide extraction, which is the same process plant roots use. This lab also gives recommendations for organic fertilization.

Nitrogen

Turfgrass requires more nitrogen than any of the other plant nutrients. It's not uncommon for the levels of nitrogen in the plant to be as much as 4 or 5 percent. Nitrogen is a part of chlorophyll and has a great deal to do with nearly all the growth and development phases in the plant.

As the amount of nitrogen supplied to the plant increases, the rate of shoot, or leaf growth, increases. This increase generally is at the expense of root growth. Rapid leaf growth tends to use up all the food material being produced by the plant, leaving very little for the roots and other organs, such as stolons or runners. It is possible to produce a lawn with very high leaf growth and a good green color but with a very restricted root system. This is one reason why minimal levels of nitrogen usually are desirable. Synthetic fertilizers all tend to be too high in nitrogen, they force-feed the plants, and they do not help biological activity and root systems at all.

High levels of nitrogen tend to produce a plant that has thin cell walls and a high water percentage in its tissue. The thickness of a cell wall may be very important when a fungus or any insect is trying to invade the plant. A plant that contains a high percentage of water requires more irrigation and is more susceptible to heat and drought stress.

The amount of nitrogen supplied to the turf plant has a great deal to do with the amount of food reserve the plant is able to store for periods of unfavorable weather, such as the period termed "winter dormancy." The plant manufactures food material, called carbohydrates, in the leaf tissue. Since the leaves have priority over the other plant parts for growth, and since nitrogen stimulates leaf growth, the oversupply of nitrogen may promote leaf growth to the point of using up all the food material the plant can supply, especially during the fall of the year. If this happens, little food material is available for storage, and the plant may not live through the winter. The goal of a good fertility program should be to produce dark-green top growth and high root growth. This is all related to heavy and balanced biological activity in the soil.

Phosphorus

Many textbooks have suggested that phosphorus is necessary for root growth. This is true, but only in the sense that it is needed for the optimum growth of all parts of the plant. Phosphorus is important to the processes of transferring and storing energy within the plant. Thus, since roots are a primary organ for energy storage, they are dependent on phosphorus. The formation and germination of the seed also creates a high demand for phosphorus. A high level of energy must be stored in the seed so that it can survive until it can germinate.

Since turf plants usually are not maintained for their seed production, their need for phosphorus is rather low, which should be reflected in the type of fertilizer used. The exception to this rule, however, is that a fertilizer containing higher levels of phosphorus is suggested when a turf is to be established from seed, sod, or sprigs. Phosphorus is an element that moves very slowly in the soil, so slowly that it may take years to move just a few inches. The speed of movement depends on the amount of clay in the soil: the higher the clay content, the slower the phosphorus moves. This movement, combined with the relatively high demand for phosphorus when you first establish a lawn, makes it highly desirable to incorporate a fertilizer with an N-P-K ratio of 1-1-1 or 1-2-2 in the soil before planting.

Many soil test reports from university labs advise using no phosphorus at all. Here's how it tends to go: Your soil test says "Warning, warning—too much phosphorus." So the advice is: Don't use a fertilizer that contains phosphorus or manure for three to five years. Well, to that I say . . . manure! The Texas A&M soil test is at best faulty in its readings and recommendations especially related to soil phosphorus. If there are phosphorus problems in your soil, it's most likely that their fertilizer recommendations in the past are the culprits. Here's the whole story and the solution to the problem—and it's organic, of course.

Back in the early nineties, a local extension agent called me about an upcoming change in A&M's fertilizer recommendations. Having finally acknowledged what the organic practitioners had known and been talking about for some time, the recently enlightened researcher was now advising using less fertilizer in general, considerably less nitrogen, no phosphorus, and no potassium. Yes, it was the first 1-0-0 (nitrogen-only) recommendation.

The alleged reasoning was that soil contained enough phosphorus and potassium. My first question was, what are the fertilizer manufacturers and others vested in the often-pushed 3-2-2 and 4-1-2 ratio products going to say? All I got was a smile and a shrug. It was good news to a degree. A&M was admitting that its long-used recommendations had been ill-advised; excess nutrients had contaminated the soil; and because of the synthetic products' solubility, the water tables, lakes, and streams had been contaminated.

Without my knowledge, one of the A&M extension people had contacted my organic friend Malcolm Beck about the looming change and talked him into producing an organic version of the 1-0-0 idea. That was the birth of his company's 9-1-1 fertilizer. My warning about being careful not to waste your time fell on deaf ears at the time, and then the expected happened. The monumental change toward a more prudent fertilizer program died on the vine. Apparently the status quo guys had more power than those trying to make improvements.

The recommendation resurfaced in 2003. The 1-0-0 idea was again the rage, at least in the minds of those pushing the idea. This time the proponents lined up in agreement. Several companies had their versions of the "new" analysis ready to go. Their reason was different this go-round. Now the alleged cause of the change was the fact that the soil has too much phosphorus and none is needed in the fertilizer applications. Potassium had been eliminated again. Just collateral damage, I suppose.

As had been briefly mentioned in the early nineties, getting a soil test before you bought fertilizer was advised, but what you should expect to find from the soil test report is that a 1-0-0 ratio nitrogen-only fertilizer is probably the product to use.

A friend of mine had been in on this conversation longer than I had. The late K Chandler had been warning educators, researchers, and farmers that not only were the recommended solutions wrong, more importantly the premise was wrong. K had been trying to explain to those involved with the A&M soil test lab that the new recommendation based on their test was wrong. The A&M soil test was one of a kind at the time. No other testing lab in the country used this particular harsh acid extraction procedure. Its fault was that it breaks the soil down completely, which shows the total nutrient content of the soil but gives no information at all about the availability of those nutrients to the plants. Today they use a slightly weaker acid, but it is still a bad test. K discovered this problem while struggling with the accuracy of his own soil tests at TPSL. He also did plant tissue tests and could never get his soil tests and tissue tests to calibrate. Then it dawned on him. How do plant roots extract nutrients from the soil? They use carbon dioxide and carbonic acid, a weak extraction acid as opposed to the harsh A&M choice. Now his tests calibrated, and since then his fertilizer recommendations have been far more helpful to growers. TPSL's tests are still the best today.

How do the two stories relate? Most of the soils showing high levels of phosphorus in the A&M test show moderate to low levels of phosphorus being available to plants in the TPSL report. Another problem with the A&M lab test is that it does not report on organic matter. As most of you already know, organic matter and carbon are essential to biological activity and nutrient availability. A&M used to stamp your report with red ink from a rubber stamp if you specifically requested that organic levels be included; now they don't even do that.

Some soils do actually have high amounts of phosphorus, but the answer is not the use of an unbalanced, carbon-free, trace-mineral-lacking, harsh synthetic nitrogen-only salt product such as 24-0-0. Fertilizers with only nitrogen will show some artificial results when first used and then harm the soil and plant growth severely in the long term. Even high-phosphorus soils need some and also potassium in the feeding program.

On the other hand, the best way to release the tied-up phosphorus in the soil is to use compost-based fertilizers: aerated compost tea, molasses, humate, Garrett Juice, and low application levels of sulfur. Another great product, from Green Industries, is Redox.

Corn gluten meal has been mentioned as a 1-0-0 analyzed organic fertilizer, but it really isn't. The true analysis of corn gluten meal is about 10-1-1 or slightly less. Actually, there is about ½ percent each of phosphorus and potassium in the product, which makes the product much better. Which reminds me—why did potassium get picked on in this new recommendation? The explanation must be really bad!

Potassium

Many plant-growth experts consider potassium to be the plant nutrient that has been passed over and not given proper credit for the role it plays in plant growth. Part of the problem is that the way potassium functions is not well understood, whereas the functions of other nutrients, such as nitrogen and phosphorus, have been more clearly defined. Potassium seems to be involved in many growth processes, but its most important role has to do with water relations within the plant.

The absence of adequate amounts of potassium tends to produce a plant with thin cell walls and high water content, the same characteristics produced by high levels of nitrogen. As the amount of potassium supplied to the plant is increased in relationship to the level of nitrogen, cell walls become thicker and the water content of the plant drops. This makes the plant more stress tolerant and less susceptible to invasion of a disease or an insect attack.

Potassium has a great deal to do with the balance in the plant between leaf and root growth. As the level of potassium supplied to the plant is increased in relationship to the level of nitrogen, the rate of leaf growth tends to be reduced. With this reduced demand for food material by the leaves, more food then becomes available for stolon, rhizome, and root growth.

Potassium is considered to be the most leachable of the plant nutrients and must be supplied at a rather constant rate. It may even be lost from the plant through its leaves during a rain or when watering.

The use of fertilizers with relatively high levels of potassium has been hard to "sell" because, unlike other nutrients, its use does not necessarily result in a change that is easy to measure. Research has shown, however, that when potassium is supplied in optimum levels, the turf plant is less susceptible to such factors as drought, heat, cold, and disease.

Fertilizer Ratios and Analysis

Several factors are used to determine the best ratio of nitrogen, phosphorus, and potassium for a turf fertilizer: the functions of each nutrient in the plant, the amount of each nutrient required by the plant, and the relationship between each nutrient in the growth of the plant. Putting these factors all together, research has shown that the best N-P-K ratio for turf establishment is 1-1-1 or 1-2-2. For a mature, established turf, the best N-P-K ratio seems to be 3-1-2 or 4-1-2. With organic fertilizers, these numbers aren't critical.

Yearly Fertilizer Needed

The grasses used for lawns vary in the amount of fertilizer they need for optimum growth during the year. Because of the wide variety of fertilizer ratios available, application rates usually are expressed as pounds of nitrogen (the first number in the analysis) per 1,000 square feet.

Application Rate and Timing

Both the rate at which a fertilizer is applied to a lawn and the interval between applications has a great deal to do with the form of nitrogen used in the fertilizer. It generally is recommended that a quickly available nitrogen fertilizer not be applied at a rate any greater than 1 pound of actual nitrogen per 1,000 square feet per application. To find out how much of a given fertilizer it takes to have a pound of nitrogen, simply divide the first number of the analysis (the percentage of nitrogen) into 100. For example, if the fertilizer has a 15-5-10 analysis, 15 goes into 100 about seven times, so 7 pounds of 15-5-10 contains 1 pound of nitrogen. The slowly available material may be applied at higher rates. However, you really don't need to worry about these numbers when using organic fertilizers.

The synthetic fertilizer proponents say that lawns should not be fertilized during periods of dormancy or during stress periods. Dormancy occurs during the winter for the warm-season grasses such as Bermudagrass, St. Augustinegrass, buffalograss, and centipedegrass. It occurs during the summer for the cool-season grasses. They say that the first application of fertilizer on lawns should be made in the spring after they have "greened up." The last application should be made in the fall. The truth about organic fertilizers is that they can be applied any month of the year.

An organic fertilizer should be used on St. Augustinegrass during the summer months to reduce the chance of disease or insect damage. St. Augustinegrass may, from time to time, suffer from chlorosis. Applications of iron sulfate or iron chelate at the manufacturer's direction are commonly recommended by those still using synthetic fertilizers, but there is a much more effective solution. Organic fertilizers contain many trace minerals that will often eliminate the problems, and greensand is a naturally mined material that contains a wide range of trace minerals and a large concentration of plant-available iron.

The cool-season grasses, such as tall fescue and bluegrass, should be fertilized during their active growth periods in the spring and fall but not during periods when they are under stress, such as during the hot weather of the summer. This is especially the case in the warmer zones that can grow these grasses.

Methods of Application

Organic fertilizer can best be applied with a "cyclone"- or "whirlybird"-type spreader. These are also called "broadcast" spreaders. There are also drop-type spreaders, but they are not very efficient and often cause streaking because of overlap of the pattern. Proper distribution with those machines is very difficult. Dark and light stripes or areas will appear in the lawn as a result of an uneven fertilizer application. This can happen somewhat with the broadcast spreaders as well, but to a lesser degree. This uneven color problem is much more of an issue with synthetic fertilizers than with the organic choices. The best way to prevent this problem in either case is to divide the total amount of fertilizer needed for the lawn into two equal amounts. Using the broadcast spreader for best results, apply one-half of the total in one direction and the rest at right angles to the first application.

Why a Fertilizer Burns

One of the bad characteristics of soluble nitrogen fertilizer is the potential for "burning" turfgrasses. The risk of fertilizer burn is one of the reasons why there has been a shift to nitrogen fertilizers that contain a high percentage of slowly soluble nitrogen instead of totally soluble nitrogen. Once again, organic fertilizers completely avoid this problem because they are totally slow release.

Fertilizers are salts not unlike table salt except that they contain various plant nutrients. When a salt is added to water, the osmotic pressure of the solution is increased. Osmotic pressure is a measure of how tightly water is held in a solution. When a synthetic fertilizer, either as a solid or a liquid, is applied to the surface of the soil, the salts must eventually enter and become a part of the soil solution (the water part of the soil) before the nutrients can enter the roots and be used by the turfgrass plant. The increase in the osmotic pressure of the soil solution associated with the application of a fertilizer may determine whether the plant will survive or will die from a fertilizer burn.

For a plant's root system to take in water, the water must pass through a root cell membrane. Water can pass through this membrane only when the osmotic pressure of the solution inside the cell is higher than the osmotic pressure of the soil solution outside the cell. Water moves from a solution with low osmotic pressure into a solution with higher osmotic pressure. If the osmotic pressure of the soil solution becomes higher than that of the solution inside the cell, water cannot enter the cell and may even move out of it. This results in the death of the cell. When root cells die, the whole plant may die. The end result is termed a "fertilizer burn."

An understanding of the potential salt effect of the various fertilizer materials can help prevent possible fertilizer burn. Salt index values are a measure of a material's relative tendency to increase the osmotic pressure of the soil solution as compared with the increase caused by an equal weight of sodium nitrate. The salt index of sodium nitrate is 100. The higher the salt index, the greater the potential of material to increase the osmotic pressure of the soil solution and thus the potential for burn.

Nitrogen is applied on a unit basis (i.e., per 1,000 square feet). Although a material such as ammonium sulfate has a lower salt index than urea, the salt effect of applied urea is lower because it contains a higher percentage of nitrogen.

The potential for burn does not depend totally on the salt index of the fertilizer material. The moisture status of the soil and of the turfgrass plant is also important. If the level of the soil solutions is low, a fertilizer will have a greater effect on increasing the osmotic pressure of the soil solution. When a fertilizer is "watered in," the volume of the soil solution increases and thus the osmotic pressure of the soil solution is reduced. In well-drained soils, however, heavy applications of water, while having the beneficial effect of reducing the osmotic pressure of the soil solution, may also have the harmful effect of leaching nutrients past the root system.

Both the air temperature and the humidity affect the water status of the plant, which is the amount of water in the air surrounding the plant. These factors to a large degree affect the plant's water requirements. As the air temperature increases, the plant requires more water, and as the humidity decreases, the plant requires more water. As the osmotic pressure of the soil solution increases, less and less water is available to the plant. Watering in a fertilizer material may increase the water available to the root system by decreasing the osmotic pressure of the soil solution, but it may also aid in reducing the plant's water requirements by cooling the plant and increasing the humidity of the plant's environment. Soluble fertilizer materials may be used at any time of the year with minimal risk of damage to turf if the factors that contribute to a burn are understood. The salt index of a fertilizer material is extremely important, especially when the fertilizer is highly soluble. The rates of application must be lower when a fertilizer with a high salt index is used, basically because of the salt effect.

Fertilizers with a low salt index should be used when soil test results indicate the presence of excessive levels of soluble salts in the soil. This can be a real problem in many areas. All plants react to salt problems just as the grass plant does.

The common theme you will notice throughout this book is that the organic program, for the most part, avoids all these problem issues. The organic products don't produce salt contaminations and have great buffering powers if anything out of balance is applied. Knowing about the salt issues as explained above is good, but in reality, organic gardeners and contractors don't have to worry about those details in most cases.

Why Are Weed-and-Feed Fertilizers So Bad?

Weed-and-feed products are a combination of herbicide chemicals and fertilizer chemicals in the same bag. The first problem is that the two ingredients aren't designed to be applied at the same time. Application timing for preemergent herbicides isn't the proper timing for application of the soluble synthetic fertilizers. The second problem is that these products will damage and/or kill your trees, shrubs, and other untargeted products as well. That makes the product even more toxic. This warning is usually on the label, but of course most people don't read the labels. These products contain preemergent herbicides, which kill young sprouting weeds, or postemergent herbicides, which kill grown weed plants. Some of the ingredients, such as atrazine in the popular Scotts Bonus S, are severely damaging to trees. Again, it says so on the bag. Some weed-and-feed mixtures also contain other pesticides such as insecticides and fungicides. The attraction of weed-and-feed fertilizers is that they cut down on lawn-care time by giving you everything you need in one bag. But they create a fraudulent perception. Rather than solving all your lawn problems, these products contaminate the soil, stress plants, and cause even more difficulties. Do you reckon the aim is to sell you some other toxic chemical products promising to solve the problems the first chemical products created?

Applying herbicide all over your lawn is overkill when you only have isolated weeds, and the chemicals can damage the environment. Applying fertilizer, herbicide, and pesticide more precisely, when they are needed, is a better lawn-care strategy—especially when organic techniques are used.

Chemical Fertilizing Summary

- Don't use synthetic fertilizer, and never use weed-and-feed products.
- Do not apply organic fertilizer more that 3 times a year.
- Foliar-feed plants with liquid organic products such as Garrett Juice at least quarterly.
- Apply compost at ½" to the entire lawn in the fall—at least for the first two years, and any time later if the turf is in stress.

Fertilizing the Lawn the Natural Way

The natural way to fertilize is to feed the soil and let the healthy soil feed the plants. Creating biological activity is the goal. Microbe poop and dead bodies of microbes are the true natural fertilizers for the soil and the plant roots. Those are created in healthy soils and sped up by quality organic fertilizers and amendments. Organic fertilizers should be applied two to three times per year at 20 pounds per 1,000 square feet or whatever the label recommends. During the growing season, spray turf monthly with compost tea, molasses, apple cider vinegar, seaweed, and fish mix (Garrett Juice). Add volcanic and other rock mineral sands once every two to ten years at 40–80 pounds per 1,000 square feet. Apply beneficial bacteria and mycorrhizal fungus products at least once a year. In a perfect world with clean air and water, a onetime inoculation would be enough, but unfortunately that's not the world we live in, so nature needs a little help from us.

There are many problems with synthetic fertilizers, but one of the biggest problems is that they contain no organic matter and therefore no carbon. Soil microorganisms must have this carbon energy source, and if it is not provided, the microbes will take it from the soil. That causes soil health reduction with every fertilizer application.

Organic fertilizers nourish and improve the soil with every application. Unlike synthetic fertilizers, they help the soil because they do not create high levels of salts and nitrates in the soil, which kill or repel beneficial soil organisms. Organic fertilizers release nutrients slowly and naturally. All components in an organic fertilizer are usable by the plants, since there are no useless or toxic fillers as there are in many synthetic fertilizers.

The nitrogen-phosphorus-potassium analysis (N-P-K) printed on bags of fertilizer by law is basically irrelevant in an organic program. Feeding the soil and plants with nothing but nitrogen, phosphorus, and potassium is like feeding your kids nothing but cheese. Soil and people need a balance of vitamins and minerals. For some unknown reason, fertilizer recommendations continue to emphasize these three nutrients with special emphasis on high levels of nitrogen. A standard obsolete recommendation is a ratio of 3-1-2 or 4-1-2, such as 15-4-10 or 16-4-8. Compost, the most natural fertilizer in the world, has an analysis of less than 1-1-1 in most cases.

A large percentage of synthetic nitrogen applied to the soil will be leached out, and what does reach the plant is harmful. Fast-acting artificial fertilizer creates weak, watery cells, a condition that invites insects and diseases. Harsh synthetic fertilizer slows or even stops the activity of microflora and microfauna such as beneficial bacteria, algae, fungi, and other microorganisms. Harsh fertilizers also cause damage to macroorganisms, such as earthworms, millipedes, centipedes, and others, which are extremely important to the natural processes in the soil.

High-nitrogen fertilizers can also cause severe thatch buildup in lawns by forcing unnatural flushes of green growth. That's why mechanical thatch-removal programs are often recommended for chemically maintained lawns. Organic lawn-care programs take care of thatch problems naturally as the living microorganisms feed on the grass clippings and other dead organic matter.

High-nitrogen fertilizers such as 15-5-10 (or even higher) are still being recommended by many in the farming, ranching, and landscaping businesses. I've made the same recommendations myself in the past, but those amounts of nitrogen, phosphorus, and potassium are unnecessary and even damaging to soil health.

When healthy, the soil will produce and release nutrients during the decomposition process. The microbiotic activity releases tied-up trace elements such as iron, zinc, boron, chlorine, copper, magnesium, molybdenum, and others, which are all important to a well-balanced soil.

The most important material in an organic program is organic matter, which is the vast array of carbon compounds in the soil that become humus during the decomposition process. Humus contains humic acid, other beneficial acids, enzymes, and mineral nutrients.

Organic fertilizers are better than artificial products because they are the derivatives of plants and therefore contain most or all of the trace elements that exist in growing plants. Synthetic fertilizers do not have this rounded balance of mineral nutrients. They are not close to being complete and balanced as is advertised. The most important missing link is carbon. It may be the most important fertilizer element, but it's totally ignored in the artificial fertilizers.

In addition, organic fertilizers are naturally slow release and provide nutrients to plants when they need them. Synthetic fertilizers glut the plants with nutrients immediately after application or soon thereafter, which is usually at the wrong time.

Human-made chemical fertilizers always have a high total N-P-K, from 20 to 60 percent or more. The total N-P-K of organic fertilizer blends will always be low, usually no higher than 14 percent.

What's in the bag other than N-P-K? The balance of the ingredients in the chemical fertilizer bag, aside from the total N-P-K, is usually inert filler or possibly other chemical elements that aren't needed or may even be toxic waste materials. The balance of the ingredients in the organic fertilizer bag beyond the total N-P-K are all necessary nutrients, enzymes, microbes, and organic matter. Organic ingredients are materials that came from living organisms—plants, animals, or a blend of both. Every ingredient is important and is buffered with organic material to work efficiently to naturally feed the life in the soil. The only other ingredients in natural fertilizers are the rock minerals that help hold water and feed microorganisms to help build healthy soil.

Many synthetic fertilizers are labeled "complete," but that's a false statement. More than a few chemicals are needed to maintain healthy soil and grow healthy plants. For example, there is little if any carbon in a bag of synthetic fertilizer. When a plant or animal body is analyzed, one of the most abundant elements in it is carbon, in the form of carbohydrates.

For a plant to be properly fed, whether with synthetic or natural fertilizer, the microbial life in the soil must first process it and release it in the correct amounts that are perfect for the plant to use. In order for the microbes to perform this service, they must have energy. They are not in the presence of sunlight, nor do they have chlorophyll like higher plants, so the microbes must get their energy from decaying plant or animal matter in the soil.

A bag of organic fertilizer has all the carbon energy to meet the needs of the soil microbes. A bag of synthetic fertilizer usually has no carbon energy. If organic matter is not already present in the soil, the chemicals can quickly become stressful, even toxic, to the plants. This causes plants to be susceptible to disease and insect problems. Unbalanced high-nitrogen fertilizers are one of the primary causes of insect and disease infestations.

Organic fertilizers are believed to be slower acting than the synthetics. This is true to a degree, but it's not a bad thing. Having a lower N-P-K analysis and slower action, organic fertilizers can be used in higher volumes around plants without danger of burning them. However, there are some organic fertilizers that are fast acting. Bat guano and fish meal can show results as quickly as the chemical fertilizers, but they are still slower to burn than synthetics and last much longer in the soil. Although certain specific organic nutrients work slower than salt nutrients, the overall organic program is not slow. When done properly, the organic program produces healthy growth and good color during the very first growing season.

Very small percentages of salt fertilizers get into the targeted plants. First of all, a significant percentage of the products volatilize into the air, adding to air pollution. Unless synthetic fertilizers are impregnated or coated with a microbe inhibitor or some substance to keep them from quickly dissolving, they must be used very cautiously, especially in sandy soils, because they can burn the plants' roots then quickly leach beyond the reach of the roots. They generally end up harming the soil and polluting the water supply because they are too quickly dissolved and move rapidly through the soil. This is less a problem in heavy clay soils or any soil with a high organic and humus content. Synthetic fertilizer N-P-K is just that, a pure synthetic form of nitrogen, phosphorus, and potassium with possibly some form of trace or minor elements blended in. Most are highly soluble and can leach past the roots into the water table to pollute well water or run off into streams.

Synthetic fertilizers are blended to force-feed plants to give quick color and growth. They do not build healthy plants, and they for sure do not build or sustain a healthy soil.

Organic fertilizers contain the carbon energy and trace minerals that continually build soil fertility, crumb structure, water-holding capacity, and food for all the beneficial soil life. They all condition the soil and contribute to the hundreds of other yet-unknown things that cause a plant to grow healthy and perfect.

High-nitrogen synthetic fertilizers have other problems. They use a bad source of phosphorus that ties up trace minerals and other nutrients, making them inaccessible to plants. Triple superphosphate is the culprit (0-46-0). It is used because it's cheap. Unfortunately for our soils, it has caused huge problems with the health of many soils. Potash is also a problem in synthetic fertilizers. It is often potassium chloride (KCl), and chloride is harmful to the soil.

High-nitrogen fertilizers such as 15-5-10 (or even higher) are still being recommended by many in the turf business. These amounts of nitrogen, phosphorus, and potassium are unnecessary and damaging to soil health.

Synthetic fertilizers are fast-acting short-term plant growth enhancers and are responsible for several problems: (1) deterioration of soil structure, creating hardpan soil; (2) destruction of beneficial soil life, including earthworms; (3) changing nutrient and vitamin content of certain crops; (4) making grasses more susceptible to diseases and insect pests; (5) preventing plants from absorbing needed minerals.

Foliar Feeding

Foliar feeding is a method of fertilizing through the foliage of plants with a liquid spray. A mixture of liquid seaweed and fish emulsion is the most common recommendation given by organic practitioners, but there is actually a better recommendation now. It is Garrett Juice, which is a mixture of compost tea or liquid humate, natural vinegar, molasses, and seaweed.

Foliar feeding has been used since 1944 when it was discovered that plant nutrients could be leached from leaves by rain. Experiments soon proved that nutrients could also enter the plant through the foliage. It still is somewhat of a mystery as to exactly how the nutrients enter the plants through the foliage—whether it is through the stomata or right through the cuticle of the leaves—but it is agreed that it works and it works quickly and efficiently.

Dr. T. L. Senn of Clemson University wrote about foliar feeding in detail in his book *Seaweed and Plant Growth*, in which he explains the powers of seaweed as a fertilizer and root stimulator and how foliar feeding can be used to supplement a fertilization program as well as help control certain plant pests such as spider mites and other small insects. Foliar feeding is several hundred times more efficient than soil fertilization according to Dr. Senn, and organic foliar sprays are the most effective, since the nutrients are in a more balanced proportion for plant growth.

Foliar sprays of organic products activate plant growth and flower and fruit production by increasing the photosynthesis in the foliage, increasing the translocation of fluids and energy within the plant, stimulating microorganisms in the soil, and increasing the uptake of soil nutrients through the root hairs. Foliar feeding increases the efficiency of all the natural systems in the soil and plants. The end result is a bigger, stronger, healthier plant with increased drought and pest resistance.

Here are some points to remember when using foliar sprays:

- Less is usually better in foliar sprays because light, regularly applied sprays are better than heavy, infrequent blasts on plant foliage.
- Mists of liquids are better than big drops.
- Young, tender foliage absorbs nutrients better than mature, hard foliage, so it is best to foliar-feed during the periods of new growth on plants.

Garrett Juice

Trombone sprayer for
applying Garrett Juice

Power sprayer for commercial
work. Photo courtesy of
Moore Tree Care.

- Sugar and molasses added to spray solutions can stimulate the growth of beneficial microorganisms on the leaf surfaces and in the soil.
- The stimulation of friendly microbes helps to fight off harmful pathogens.
- Well-timed foliar feeding on food crops will increase their storage life.

Additionally, spraying on damp, humid mornings or cool, moist evenings increases the effectiveness of foliar sprays. The least effective time to foliar-feed is during the heat of midday. Small openings called stomata in the leaves close up during the heat of the day or as a result of other stress so moisture within the plant is preserved. The very best time to get the indirect pest control may be dusk so that the liquid stays on the plant leaves as long as possible during the night. Some would argue that this practice increases diseases, but I am not sure I agree with that. Gasses and liquids are best absorbed through the leaves during this period. The fluids that are moving down the plant and roots are at their peak during the cooler hours of the day.

The best foliar-feeding material is Garrett Juice, and the formulas for both concentrate and ready-to-use mixtures can be found in the appendix.

Basic Organic Fertilization Program for Lawns

March: Apply 100% organic granular fertilizer @ 20 lbs./1,000 sq. ft.; in alkaline soils, add lava sand @ 40 lbs./1,000 sq. ft.; and in acid soils, add high-calcium lime @ 20–30 lbs./1,000 sq. ft.

April: Spray liquid hydrolyzed fish, seaweed, molasses, and biostimulant or Garrett Juice.

June: Apply 100% organic fertilizer @ 10–15 lbs./1,000 sq. ft.

August: Spray liquid fish emulsion, seaweed, molasses, and vinegar or Garrett Juice.

September: Spray liquid hydrolyzed fish, seaweed, and biostimulant or Garrett Juice.

October: Apply 100% organic fertilizer @ 10 lbs./1,000 sq. ft.

Composting and Organic Matter

Organic matter is probably the most important and most misunderstood tool of the organic program. Organic matter serves as a reservoir of nutrients and water in the soil, aids in reducing soil compaction and surface crusting, and increases water infiltration into the soil. Organic material is anything that was alive and is now in or on the soil. Organic matter is the broken-down material we call humus. Humus is organic material that has been converted by microorganisms to a resistant state of decomposition. Organic material is unstable in the soil, changing form and mass readily as it decomposes. As much as 90 percent of it disappears quickly because of decomposition. Organic matter, or humus, on the other hand, is stable in the soil. It has been decomposed until it is resistant to further decomposition.

Benefits of Organic Matter

Organic matter has many important uses in the soil. It is a reservoir of nutrients; it is a buffering agent; and it supports biological activity, holds moisture, helps loosen the soil, and helps improve drainage. Organic matter behaves somewhat like a sponge, with the ability to absorb and hold up to 90 percent of its weight in water. A great advantage of the water-holding capacity of organic matter is that the matter will release most of the water that it absorbs to plants. In contrast, clay holds great quantities of water, but much of it is unavailable to plants.

Organic matter, because of its population of beneficial microbes, causes soil to clump and form soil aggregates, which improves soil structure, aeration, and biological health. Research indicates that increasing soil organic matter from 1 to 3 percent can reduce erosion 20 to 33 percent because of increased water infiltration and more stable soil-aggregate formation.

Compost: Mother Nature's Fertilizer

Compost is the best organic material by far. The simple definition of compost is organic matter that's broken down into an unidentifiable form. Every living thing on earth is going to die, and everything that dies, rots. Completely rotted material is compost. Compost contains many nutrients and therefore is a fertilizer—the best fertilizer on earth, since it's nature's own. Composting is also an excellent organic process for recycling waste—a bad term to use for organic matter, which is an important natural resource, not a waste by-product.

Compost comes from the Latin word *compostum*, meaning "to bring together." I like composts that are made from several different ingredients. The ideal mixture is 75–80 percent dry, brown vegetative matter and 20–25 percent animal manure and green plant material. The best composting materials are those that exist on your own property; the next best are those that are easily obtainable nearby. The location of the compost pile can be in sun or shade, and covers are not necessary (although some composters like to use covers to prevent rains from cooling the pile).

The three most common questions I get about composting are: (1) What can and cannot go in the compost pile? (2) Where should the pile be located? and (3) What kind of container should be used?

The location answer is: anywhere, sun or shade. On the ingredients question, the answer is very simple. Anything once alive can and should go in the compost pile. The only risk is attracting wild animals if meat and greasy products are left

Mycorrhizal fungus used on bentgrass seed for plants on the left but not on the right. Photo by Mike Amaranthus, courtesy of Mycorrhizal Applications, Inc.

Multispecies turf

Bentgrass

Common Bermudagrass in summer

Dormant common Bermudagrass

Bermudagrass seed heads

Tifway 419 fairways

Dormant Tifway 419 fairways

Reveille bluegrass looked beautiful when first planted.

Curious spots started to develop the first week.

It was mostly dead within a few weeks.

The phytotoxicity had been caused by *this* fido!

Dormant 609 buffalograss

Buffalograss seed

Buffalograss at the Ladybird Johnson Wildflower Center

Buffalograss seed heads

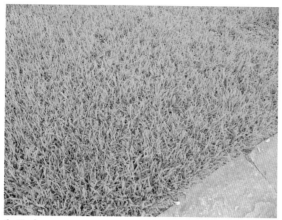

Centipedegrass

Tall fescue

Paspalum, a drought-, wear-, and salt-tolerant grass that should be used more often

Annual ryegrass

Perennial ryegrass

St. Augustinegrass

Zoysia used in between stepping stones

"Meyer" Z-52 zoysia

Result of vinegar herbicide spraying around young tree

Scalping done prior to overseeding with ryegrass in the fall

Sod that was not watered before laying

Sod properly watered on the back side before laying—a good thing. But I don't like the drip systems (as shown) used for turf irrigation.

High-nitrogen fertilizers are salts.

Shepherd Complete Composter/
Compost Bin, a wire-frame
composter with aerator
chimney—my favorite

Chinch bugs can be serious pests on stressed turf.

Fire ants like grass areas where synthetic fertilizers and pesticides are still
being used.

Beneficial nematodes—one of the
best biological pest-control tools

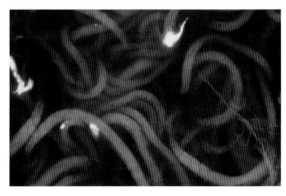

Bermuda mites—usually only an issue in stressed turf

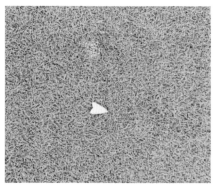

Sod webworm damage and an adult moth on bentgrass

Brown patch—a fungal disease caused by too much water and fertilizer

Fairy rings are mostly cosmetic. The mushrooms are the fruiting bodies of fungi that are feeding on decaying organic material in the soil. In this case, the roots of removed trees are the source of the fairy-ring growth.

Gray leaf spot is common on unhealthy St. Augustinegrass.

Slime mold is cosmetic only.

St. Augustine Decline (SAD)

An example of take-all patch

Corn gluten meal—a good organic fertilizer and sometimes effective preemergent herbicide

Dwarf strawberry–infested St. Augustine treated with Agralawn (cinnamon and potassium bicarbonate product)

Results after treatment: healthy St. Augustine and no weeds

Poa annua—common cool-season weed

Chickweed—cool-season weed

Bur clover

Dwarf white clover—one of the pretty weeds

Crabgrass—common summer weed

Dichondra—a so-called weed that should be encouraged. It's actually a good-looking ground cover.

Grassbur—one of the most-asked-about noxious summer weeds

Henbit in dormant turf—an easy-to-control cool-season weed

Johnsongrass—rarely a problem in turf because it cannot stand to be mowed

Nutsedge—usually referred to as nutgrass. It's hard to control, but aerating the soil helps more than anything.

Purslane—an edible weed that should be harvested instead of sprayed

Rescuegrass—common cool-season weed that is often the most prevalent weed in the late winter

Roadside aster—classic poor-soil-health weed

on the outside edge of the pile. These must be buried into the compost pile and should be mixed with high-carbon materials such as sawdust, wood shavings, or dry leaves to prevent odor and the waste of the nitrogen escaping from the pile.

The best way to neutralize old seed, weeds, diseased plants, dead insects, manure of any kind, kitchen scraps of any kind, and corpses of any kind is to compost them. Weeds and weed seed are loaded with minerals, often those that are lacking in the soil. If you want to make sure the pile heats up well and does a thorough job of neutralizing weed seed and other ingredients, add cornmeal and molasses to the pile. The amounts are not critical. Some people will tell you not to put greasy food from the kitchen in the pile. I say, if it shouldn't go in the compost pile, you sure as heck shouldn't have been eating it!

Another common question is, What about toxic contaminants such as the weed-and-feed fertilizer my neighbor used on his grass? All organic matter needs to be recycled instead of buried in a landfill even if it is contaminated. Thorough composting will probably break down the contaminants, especially if you add lots of cornmeal and molasses to the pile. Also try to talk some sense into your neighbor.

There are many good recipes for compost, but it's almost impossible to foul up the compost-making process. Even 100 percent pure vegetative matter or animal matter can be composted. Composting is as much an art as a science, and a little experimenting is good. I find that the simplest systems are usually the best. With new gardens or planting beds, the composting can be done in the beds themselves by lightly tilling raw organic matter into the soil. Once this has been done, it's best to wait at least two months to plant. Surface composting, like the composting on a forest floor, simply takes a little longer than composting in a pile.

Composting should be done whenever the raw materials are available, and compost piles should be working year-round. A convenient site, such as a utility area behind the garage, a shed, or a dog run, should be chosen for the location of the compost pile, and for greatest efficiency, it should be on a paved surface so that the leachate can be caught and used as a liquid fertilizer. The advantage of locating a compost pile on soil, however, is that although the leachate is wasted, the earthworms can enter the pile easily and help complete the composting process.

The material can be piled on the ground or in the dog run or on the driveway. Some people, however, want to be neat, while others think using a container makes better compost, and some just like to buy and build gadgets. Whatever the reason, if you need to use a container, compost bins can be made out of wooden pallets, a wood frame covered with wire mesh, corrugated tin, plastic, fiberglass, hay bales, old signs, old tires, cinder blocks, untreated lumber, or whatever else you have lying around that has a minimum volume of 3 cubic feet.

Avoid chemically treated wood, especially railroad ties, since the heavy metals in the preservative are highly toxic to both tiny and large living organisms. Store-bought compost bins are also available; they're hardly worth the cost, but it's your money. Just make sure you have plenty of space, although if you have the space, a container isn't really even necessary—just make a big pile. Even apartment dwellers, however, can make compost at home; containers made from plastic, rubber, fiberglass, and other recycled materials make excellent compost bins for people with limited space.

Hay bales make good natural building blocks to form a compost container. Stack the bales to make a two- or three-sided enclosure. The hay bales can ultimately be pulled into the mix to become part of the compost. Alfalfa is by far the best choice for two reasons: It is loaded with nutrients and it doesn't have the risk of being contaminated with recalcitrant herbicides such as picloram and clopyralid. The best compost container is the Shepherd Complete Composter. It's made of high-quality steel, folds for storage if necessary, holds a good volume of material, and is easy to manage.

Good compost ingredients include grass clippings, leaves of all kinds, sawdust, dead plants, weeds (and no, don't worry about the weed seeds), tree chips, coffee grounds, tea leaves, feathers, old bird seed, feather meal, seaweed, peanut hulls, pine cones, pecan hulls and other nut shells, fish scraps, brewery waste, slaughterhouse waste, pine needles, wool, silk, cotton, granite dust, uncooked vegetable scraps, fruit peelings, pet hair, dust, and animal manure. Some say dog and cat manure should not be used in the compost pile. I don't have cats, but I do use my dogs' manure in the piles, since a properly managed compost pile will neutralize almost all pathogens. *Many advisers say to avoid greasy, salty, and cooked foods in general. Again, I say this: If it can't go in the compost pile, you sure shouldn't have been eating it!* It is a good idea to avoid dyed or printed materials, synthetic fabrics, burned charcoal, and plastics.

Making Compost

There's lots of misinformation about composting, most of which makes the process seem too difficult. Compost creation is more of a fact than either an art or a science. All living things—plants and animals—will die and then rot to become compost. All you have to do is make a pile of previously living materials. Nature will do the rest. It's easy, but here are some points that might help your composting seem even easier.

Compost bins: Containers really aren't necessary. Heaps or piles work just fine. Mesh, lumber, shipping pallets, cinder blocks, or hay bales can be used if space is limited. Covers aren't necessary. Compost piles can be located in the shade or in full sun.

Bioactivators and other additives: Bacteria-laden powders, liquids, and special

Battery of Shepherd composters at the Coppell, Texas, community gardens

inoculants are usually unnecessary. Every piece of organic matter is naturally covered with thousands or even millions of fungi and bacteria. Yeast, sugar, and molasses will naturally serve as biostimulants if you feel it's necessary to speed up the process. Molasses is an excellent choice. Bio-S.I. is a high-quality commercial microbe product.

Worms: Adding earthworms or worm cocoons is unnecessary. If the dead material is piled and moisture is added, the biology of the compost pile will include earthworms. Molasses, dry or liquid, will attract earthworms better than any ingredient. It will also repel fire ants from the pile.

Fertilizer: Synthetic nitrogen fertilizers are unbalanced and harsh and contain excess mineral salts and other contaminants. It's legal for industrial wastes to be in synthetic fertilizers. Natural fertilizers like cottonseed meal, coffee, manures, and dried blood work well. Food products like cornmeal are also beneficial in the compost blend.

Adding calcium to raise the pH or adding iron or sulfur to lower the pH of the pile is an unnecessary waste of time. Finished compost is almost always nearly neutral. On the other hand, a very small amount of sulfur added to the pile will stimulate the feeding of the microbes and thus the heat and decomposition of the pile. However, be aware that more than 1 cup of sulfur per cubic yard will actually hurt the microbes.

Odor: Stink results from too much moisture, too much nitrogen, and not enough air. Problems can result from excess grass clippings, too many food scraps, and/or too much manure. To reduce odor, add more carbon in the form of dry leaves or sawdust and turn the pile more often to increase the oxygen.

Animals and insects: Animals like mice and rats and insects like roaches and pill bugs can become a nuisance even though they are helping break down the organic material. Bird feed, pet food, scraps from the kitchen, and the bodies of dead animals can attract hungry animals. Just make sure to put these kinds of ingredients down into the center of the pile. And yes, it is okay to put the pet waste and dead animals into the compost pile. That's exactly where they should go.

Layers: Carefully placing the ingredients into lasagna-style layers looks good in the beginning, but it's a total waste of time. Just mix all the materials together. They'll be that way after the first turning anyway.

Turning: It's optional. The pile will decompose into compost without it, but stirring or turning has two advantages. The oxygen will stimulate the faster breakdown of the raw materials, and the outside edge of the pile will be exposed to the microbe feeding of the interior.

Carbon-to-nitrogen ratios: This is too much science and math for me and most home composters. Compost piles thrive when various amounts and various types of materials are mixed together. Ratios are fine to worry about if you don't have anything else to do, but all organic materials will compost in a timely manner if given water, air, and time.

> Applying about an inch of compost to the lawn in the fall is probably the very best thing you can do for the turf.

Ants in the Compost

To get rid of ants in the compost pile, all you have to do is add cornmeal and some molasses. The ants don't like either product, but the combination of them with the other ingredients, like dry leaves, food scraps, and moisture in the pile, will run the ants out quickly and help create a better compost. Both of these amendments super-stimulate microbes in the pile. These beneficial microorganisms are the best of all fire ant controls. The ants know that fact and will scram.

Maggots in the Compost Pile

One homeowner asked me: "What about maggots in the compost pile? The pile was built on bare soil where a portable storage building was removed. A rat was buried beneath this area about two months prior to starting the pile. Could it be the cause of the maggots? They appear to be degrading everything that goes in the pile, but am I going to be fly infested as a result?"

Maggots are the larvae of a beneficial insect called the soldier fly or black soldier fly or of other beneficial insects. These worms help break down the compost materials. One of these adults is a beneficial blue-black wasplike fly that feeds on nectar and helps pollinate flowers. If you keep the compost pile soupy wet, you might see another beneficial maggot: the rat-tailed maggot, which grows up to be another pollinator—one of the hover flies—whose larvae feed on pest insects. In other words, don't worry about the maggots; their larva form helps the compost pile, and their adult form helps pollinate plants.

Roaches in the Compost

Get a grip! Roaches are not only no threat outdoors and in the compost pile, they are beneficial by feeding on and helping break down organic matter. Next, boric acid, which is used to kill roaches, should never be used outdoors because it will foul up the chemistry of the soil in a hurry. Other than that, you aren't doing anything wrong except driving yourself crazy. To make the insects less active around the compost pile, turn it more often, add dry molasses or a product that contains it, and sprinkle natural diatomaceous earth around and over the pile after turning.

Newspaper Ink

It's the black ink that is a petroleum product and more likely to contain the toxic materials such as heavy metals. The color ink is more commonly soy based and cleaner. To make sure, call your paper and asked them. It's best to compost any printed paper first instead of using it directly as a mulch and to use it only on ornamental plants.

Leaf-Mulch Composting

Another form of composting is done by simply mulching leaves into the turf. This is mostly a fall activity but a very important subject for lawns anywhere in the country. Bagging leaves is a big mistake and should be banned in all cities.

This fall practice is one of the most dramatic examples of environmental thuggery in my neighborhood, but it is quite common everywhere, unfortunately. Here's my determined attempt to pass on some common sense on this subject: Having the leaves hauled off to the landfill increases taxes, wastes time and money, throws away valuable soil-building organic material, and looks terrible.

Leaf-Management No-Nos
1. Leaves should never be raked, put in bags, and sent to the landfill.
2. Leaves should never be raked, put into piles, and set on fire.
3. Leaves should never be raked and put into the compost pile—except as a last resort.

Mulching leaves into turf—the proper leaf management

4. Leaves should never be blown onto the neighbor's property or into the streets.

Correct Leaf Management

1. Leaves should be mowed and mulched into the turf. Using a mulching mower is best but not essential. Turf can take quite a volume of leaves before there is excess. Excess leaves would be when the lawn is about to be completely covered and smothered by the ground-up leaves.

2. At the point of excess, the leaves should still be mulched on the lawn or driveway, but raked, picked up, and distributed as mulch in flower beds and vegetable gardens.

3. When no more mulch is needed in the flower and vegetable beds, the remaining leaves that have been ground up by the lawnmower can be put into the compost pile. Add dry molasses—at about 20 pounds per 1,000 square feet—to the beds and the compost pile to help the material break down and become humus more efficiently.

4. Never under any circumstances should the leaves be removed from the site. They should either be mulched or composted. All cities should outlaw the city service of picking up leaves and grass clippings. If home and business owners have to recycle the organic matter, then the landscapes are healthier, water runoff is reduced, and less tax money has to be allocated to picking up and managing leaves and other organic matter. Everybody wins!

Using Compost for Lawn Management

Compost is a wonderful basic fertilizer for turf. If all you ever applied was a quality compost, the turf would be healthy and beautiful. Some commercial residential property managers use this exact fertility program. The only problem is the handling of the bulk material needed to make the application. As a result, it tends to be more costly than using bagged organic fertilizer.

A more cost-effective approach is to apply it in the fall in problem areas of stressed turf. The only risk there is that those areas might end up looking better than the rest of the lawn. Then you are back to applying it over the entire site, but there are worse problems to have. Without question, the best solution to compacted, stressed, weak turf areas is the application of ½" of quality compost.

Another approach is to use compost tea. Technique and technology are not always thought of with regard to organic tools. But the science of organics is increasing rapidly. For example, compost is not just compost, and the same goes for compost tea. Of all the tools we use, they may be the most important.

To make quality compost tea, start with good fungus-filled compost that contains aerobic beneficial microbes, then make them multiply by feeding and aerating them with a simple aquarium pump to increase the number of many microbes, including bacteria, fungi, protozoa, flagellates, and beneficial nematodes. Typical garden soils are weakest in fungal species, and this procedure helps them greatly. Buy a pump rated for about a 50-gallon aquarium. Do not overdo the movement of tea and beat your fungus to death but provide enough oxygen to keep the tea from going anaerobic.

Air stones, also from the pet store, are used to pump air through the tea by creating lots of bubbles. When stones become stained from the tea, clean them between each batch by soaking them in hydrogen peroxide (3% solution that comes from the grocery store). Cleaning the tea maker between every tea batch is very important.

Worm castings are one of the best composts for making tea, but any quality compost will work. Compost can be put in a nylon tea bag or left loose. Larger air stones go on the bottom of the bucket. Small air stones can be put in the tea bag. Five-gallon buckets are good to use and will make about 4 gallons of tea. Add ½ ounce of liquid molasses per gallon of water to help feed the microbes. Too much molasses can destroy microbes in the tea. Look at the movement of the water to make sure you have plenty of air and water movement. Put a lid on the bucket and let it brew for six to eight hours.

The commercial alternative to compost brewing is called "extraction." It uses a physical removal process to release the microbes. No aeration is needed for this product, and it has a shelf life of five to ten days.

When molasses is used, the tea will have a sweet smell to begin with. When the molasses is used up, the aroma of the tea will change to a yeasty aroma. Remove the tea bags if used, and continue to brew the tea with the air pump running for another sixteen to twenty hours. The tea will start to deteriorate immediately after the air pump is turned off. You can prolong the life of the tea for a day by leaving the air on, but when all the food has been used up, it will deteriorate even with the air on. Never try to store your finished tea in a closed container. It will develop pressure inside and blow up.

Five gallons of tea will cover an acre of grass or other plantings. As a soil drench, 5 gallons will cover about 10,000 square feet of lawn or garden. It doesn't matter how much water you use to dilute and spread the tea.

Cultural Management

Lawn Leveling

From time to time, especially with a new lawn, it may be necessary and desirable to level the lawn by filling in the low spots. This process is done most easily in the spring, before the lawn "greens up."

The commonly used technique is to scalp the lawn to near the soil level and spread soil into the low spots. The scalping allegedly makes it easier to spread the soil. If this technique is used, the same type of soil should be used that was used for the original lawn. Sand should not be used for leveling a lawn unless the existing soil is sand. The use of the same kind of soil and the loosening of the old soil surface, if possible, should help prevent any layering. If layers are created in a soil, they tend to restrict the development of a deep root system.

My favorite way of leveling uneven lawns is to heavily core-aerate the problem area and then rake the cores from the high spots into the low ones. This "cut and fill" method works well and is cost effective.

Aerating

I used to recommend aeration at the beginning of any organic transition, but I have modified that advice. Aerating the soil does speed up the biological improvement of the soil, but it is a luxury if the budget is limited. Organic amendments and fertilizers will accomplish the same thing but just take longer. When soil gets compacted—from foot traffic, synthetic fertilizers, and so forth—oxygen can't reach the beneficial microbes that break down organic matter to enrich the soil. Physically punching holes in the ground will speed up the process. The best aerators are those that tear the ground instead of punching smooth-sided holes.

Manual and power core-aerators remove narrow sections of soil to form shallow holes. Air, water, and organic material spread into the ground through the holes, revitalizing the soil. If heavy traffic compacts the lawn severely, it's best to aerate it every spring or fall.

Compaction is a physical process that slowly reduces the amount of oxygen contained in a soil. The roots of the turfgrass plant need oxygen and, as a product of their growth process, give off carbon dioxide. Oxygen from the atmosphere moves into the soil through very small pores to get to the roots of the plant. Carbon dioxide escapes up through the soil into the atmosphere. As the soil is trafficked, the soil particles in the top inch or two are compacted so that less and less oxygen can enter the soil and less and less carbon dioxide can escape. The net result is a thinner and thinner turf until, ultimately, the soil can no longer support any turf growth at all. An amazing number of weeds can grow in these compacted soils where the grasses can't grow.

Since compaction is the result of a physical process, it takes another physical process to reduce its effects. There are machines, usually simply called "aerifiers" or "aerators," that have a number of hollow or open metal tubes called "tines" that can be used to relieve compaction. The tines are about ½ inch in diameter, and when the machine is operated, they penetrate the soil to a depth of 2 or 3 inches. As the tine is pulled up out of the soil, a core of soil is removed. These are deposited on the surface of the lawn, and after a few waterings, they will dissipate. The holes left in the lawn become an avenue for oxygen to once again penetrate deeply into the soil and for carbon dioxide to escape. Root growth around the hole is greatly increased and the vigor of plants around the hole is greatly enhanced. Thus, the greater the number of holes poked into the lawn, the greater the increase in that lawn's vigor.

The frequency at which a lawn may need to be aerated is solely dependent on the amount of traffic it receives and, to some extent, the texture of the soil under the lawn. A lawn that has no more traffic than the foot traffic associated with normal maintenance and perhaps an occasional football game may never need to be aerated. When traffic becomes heavy enough to thin out the lawn, it is time to aerate. Heavily trafficked lawns may need to be aerated at least two or three times a year.

The best time to aerate is when the lawn is actively growing, as the roots will fill the aerator holes rapidly and the lawn will recover quickly. If a lawn is aerated during its dormant period, the open holes may allow excessive loss of soil moisture. Any lawn may be aerated, regardless of the turfgrass variety.

Thatch Control

The easy method of thatch control is to use an organic program, and then there won't be a thatch problem. The healthy conditions and biological activity will control the thatch nicely. Leaves cut off by mowing are rapidly decomposed by bacteria and fungi and do not contribute to thatch.

For those continuing to use synthetic products, here is some help for you. When organic material is produced faster than it can be decomposed, the lawn develops thatch, which primarily consists of partially decomposed stem and root tissue and some living stem and root tissues that develop in the organic layer between the base of the turfgrass plant and the soil. Stem, crown, and root tissues are high in cellulose material that's very hard to decompose.

A certain amount of thatch is desirable, because it forms a cushion in the lawn to increase wear tolerance. Since most lawns are subjected to traffic, thatch helps the lawn withstand the wear and tear associated with moderate levels of traffic. Thatch also insulates the soil from high temperatures and reduces water evaporation losses from the surface of the soil. To qualify as desirable, the thatch layer should not exceed about ¼ inch. When thatch accumulates thicker than that, problems develop. Heavy thatch layers will reduce water movement into the soil. They also reduce soil aeration, which is necessary for good root growth. Increased disease and insect problems are often associated with heavy thatch layers. Thatch layers in excess of ¼ inch can create barriers for the movement of fertilizer and insect-control products into the soil.

Some lawns tend to develop thatch fairly easily, and some do not. One reason is that turfgrasses vary in their tendency to develop thatch. There are several basic causes for thatch buildup in a lawn. Improper use of water can encourage a problem, and lawns that are excessively watered, especially those watered daily, tend to develop heavy thatch. Heavy use of pesticides on a lawn may also promote thatch accumulation by destroying many of the beneficial organisms that decompose thatch.

The major cause of thatch buildup is the use of high rates of soluble nitrogen fertilizers. Nitrogen is a plant nutrient that stimulates vegetative growth of the turfgrass. In an ideal lawn management system, the growth rate of the lawn should equal the rate at which the turfgrass residues decompose. Because of the strong influence of soluble nitrogen on growth, excessive application rates add plant residues to the system faster than they can decompose. As a result, thatch accumulates in the lawn. In addition, high-nitrogen fertilizers actually damage the beneficial microbes.

Improper mowing can also lead to thatch problems. Lawns should be mowed when the height of the grass is about one and a half times greater than the height setting of the mower. That is, if the mower is set for 2 inches, the lawn should be cut when it is no higher than 3 inches. This practice fits the basic "rule of thumb" for mowing that states "no more than one-third of the leaf surface area should be removed at one time." If a lawn is mowed at the right frequency, the clippings may be left to fall back into the turf and they will decompose rapidly. The frequency at which a lawn should be mowed is determined by the growth rate. The use of a mulching mower may help prevent a problem. While a mulching mower will not reduce the mowing frequency, it may speed up the rate at which leaf tissue decomposes. By chopping up the leaves into smaller particles, microbes have a greater surface area on which to feed.

Lawns that have too much thatch are spongy. Mowers tend to scalp lawns that have excessive thatch. To estimate the depth of thatch, use a knife or spade to remove a small section of turf. Make sure the cut extends deep enough to go through the thatch layer to the true surface of the soil. Measure the amount of thatch. If it is thicker than ¼ inch, the lawn should be dethatched. Of course, there's a bad way and a good way to do that work.

The bad way is this. Machines specifically designed for the removal of thatch are called vertical mowers (because the blades rotate vertically), power rakes, or dethatching mowers. In using this type of equipment, the blades or knives penetrate through the thatch to the surface of the soil. On St. Augustine lawns, the knives are spaced 2 or 3 inches apart; on Bermudagrass lawns, they may be 1 to 1½ inches apart. The lawn is usually vertically mowed in two directions, each time removing the material brought up by the mower by catching it in a bagging mower or raking it.

Another bad means of thatch control is to lower the height of the lawn mower's blade for the first cutting in the spring and mowing the lawn in several directions, removing the dead material after each mowing. Scalping the lawn in this manner is not as effective as using a vertical aerator mower. Consider using any thatch picked up from the lawn in a compost pile rather than adding it to already overcrowded landfills.

The proper way to accomplish dethatching is the program I recommend to loosen compacted soils. Both thatched turf and heavily compacted soil will benefit greatly from physical core aeration, or "ripping," which is tearing lines in the ground with machines that pull knifelike attachments through the soil at various depths. It's the best way to aerate but not very practical for homeowners. It is mostly used for commercial agricultural properties. Ripping the soil is actually more beneficial at aerating than poking holes, but it shouldn't be done if trees exist, as it will tear the trees' feeder roots.

The liquid aeration treatment would be to spray or drench the lawn with hydrogen peroxide. Applying the 3 percent product from the drug or grocery store is one way to go. It can be applied full strength or mixed with water 50-50. Commercial 35 percent hydrogen peroxide is also available and can be mixed at about 1 ounce per gallon of water, but this concentrated product can burn skin and eyes, so it must be handled very carefully. The ideal approach would be to do both. The physically aerated soil lets the liquid penetrate more deeply to flocculate and help loosen the soil more effectively. Apply the Garrett Juice mixture or at least compost tea after the hydrogen peroxide application and you will have fertilized the soil as well as aerated it.

Our dog Hannah used to do this to our lawn—but there is a solution.

All this work is usually a onetime need, unless the soil is physically compacted all over again.

Dog Damage to Turf

Our wonderful dogs sometimes do serious damage to lawns basically in three ways—well, at least three ways. The first is compaction of soils due to them being allowed to run in the same areas over and over. This results from leaving dogs out in backyards to run as they please. Dogs are very predictable. They run back and forth in the same place or places and compact the soil until the grass is dead. I get lots of e-mails and calls about how to correct this damage. There is only one solution—get the dogs off the turf. Dog runs are the answer, and they are not inhumane. In fact, dogs love to hang around in their outdoor rooms and then be let out to play with you and the kids on the grass while you are with them. Then they don't run nervously back and forth on the grass in the exact same spots. Best dog run to leave them in during the day? A fenced one of smooth concrete. It's good for their feet and nails and easy to keep clean.

The second problem is the pet waste killing the grass. This can be somewhat of an issue even if you follow my advice above. Solid waste should be picked up regularly and put into the compost pile. Leaving it out leads to the development of blood-sucking flies that attack the ears of pets. And no—dog poop is not a problem in the compost. That's what should be done with it. Urine, especially from female dogs, is even more damaging to grass. To prevent burned spots, the urine needs to be diluted with water quickly, but lack of time usually prevents that solution. To treat the damaged spots, apply a sprinkling of zeolite. It absorbs the ammonia and helps the damaged areas heal.

A third problem is digging. Some dogs like to dig holes in garden beds and in the turf. The solution that works sounds a little gross, but it solves the problem. Soak some of the dog's poop in a 5-gallon bucket of water and make a manure tea. Then pour the tea over the area where digging is being done. At the worst, the dogs will go somewhere else. People can smell the tea at first, but it dissipates quickly. Dogs can smell it a lot longer and stay away from it. After a week or so, it may have to be reapplied.

Pest Management

Getting rid of all the bugs, beetles, and critters in the turf is impossible. It's also a bad idea because most of these living organisms are beneficial. Insects usually do a great job of controlling themselves if we don't foul up the balance by spraying toxic pesticides, using harsh salt fertilizers, or watering too much or too little.

Insect Control

Pest control is similar to weed control. If you have a healthy, thriving lawn, you won't have many insect or disease issues. There will be lots of different insects, many very small, but most of them will be beneficial, and it would be a total waste of time to try to control them.

From time to time, however, bugs may damage some of your grass. You can treat infestations by spraying organic insecticides when necessary. Try to use insecticides that kill harmful insects specifically. Ants and spiders prey on lawn pests, so you certainly want to keep at least some of them around. The following are some of the most common insect pests in turf.

Armyworms—1½" caterpillars with stripes down the side of body
Economic Importance: Destruction to plant foliage and entire plants in some cases. Especially destructive to young grass seedlings.
Natural Control: Parasitic wasps such as trichogramma, parasitic flies, and ground beetles.

Organic Control: Release trichogramma wasps in the spring. *Bacillus thuringiensis* (Bt) products, citrus and neem products.

Bermuda Mites—tiny and visible only as the damage they cause; fairly rare
Feeding Habits: Both nymphs and adults pierce plant cells and suck juice, causing a thickening of the shoots and shortening of the internodes.
Economic Importance: Damaged grass appears pale and stunted.
Natural Control: Increased moisture in the soil.
Organic Control: Essential-oil sprays are effective. Beneficial nematodes and related soil life is the best control.

Chiggers (Red Bugs)—microscopic arachnids that cause red spots and itching
Feeding Habits: Larvae attach to skin of various animals to feed.
Economic Importance: Cause severe itching and small reddish welts on skin.
Natural Control: Increased soil moisture. Some researchers say chiggers have no natural enemies. That may be true, but the imported fire ants will certainly eliminate them.
Organic Control: Sulfur dust is a good repellent. So is lemon mint, also called horsemint, *Monarda citriodora*. Take a hot, soapy bath to remove larvae. Stop the itching with baking soda, vinegar, aloe vera, or comfrey juice.

Chinch Bugs—small white bugs that primarily attack St. Augustine
Feeding Habits: They feed the most in summer and early fall, sucking the juice from grass leaves through needlelike beaks. They inject toxic saliva into the plant that causes wilting. Most damage is caused by the nymphs and shows up in circular patterns. They like hot conditions and stressed turf.
Economic Importance: Turf damage. Foliage turns yellow, then brown, and then dies. Almost never a problem in well-maintained turf.
Natural Control: Healthy soil and turf. When weather turns cool in the fall, a beneficial fungus called *Beauveria* spp. moves in and kills these pests. It appears as a grayish cottony mass of fungal hyphae. Keep lawns moist and don't overfertilize. Big-eyed bugs are a natural enemy. Apply beneficial nematodes and big-eyed bugs as needed.
Organic Control: Diatomaceous earth and compost, manure tea, molasses, and essential-oil spray.

Crickets—brown, noisy, and destructive insects
Feeding Habits: Eat several kinds of plants, especially seedlings, including turfgrasses.
Economic Importance: Keeping people awake at night and seedling damage.
Natural Control: Birds and naturally occurring microbes.

Fire ants are easy to control with the Basic Organic Program.

Organic Control: *Nosema locustae* products, diatomaceous earth products, essential-oil sprays.

Cutworms—brown grubworm-looking caterpillars

Feeding Habits: Cut off young seedlings at ground level. Some will climb up plants and chew foliage as armyworms do.

Economic Importance: Several species of cutworms can damage small grains, tomatoes, peppers, eggplant, and cabbage.

Natural Control: Trichogramma wasps, birds, frogs, fire ants, and beneficial nematodes.

Organic Control: Diatomaceous earth or *Bacillus thuringiensis* products. Release beneficial nematodes in the spring.

Fire Ants

Feeding Habits: Omnivorous, will feed on almost any animal or plant. They eat other insects, oils, sugars, and young seedlings and saplings.

Economic Importance: Despite the damage they cause, they do have a beneficial side. They eat ticks, chiggers, termites, boll weevils, flea hoppers, cotton bollworms, pink bollworms, tobacco budworms, pecan weevils, hickory shuckworms, flies, fleas, cockroaches, and corn earworms.

Natural Control: Lizards, birds, other insects, and microorganisms.

Grubworms are the larvae of June beetles and other beetles.

Organic Control: Apply dry molasses, beneficial nematodes, and diatomaceous earth. Spraying products that contain molasses helps keep them away. Applying orange and grapefruit rind pulp to the mounds is another excellent control.

June Beetles (Grubs, Grubworms)—C-shaped soil-dwelling worms

Feeding Habits: Larvae feed on plant roots or decaying organic matter. Feeding decreases as soil temperatures decrease in the fall, when the grubs migrate deeper into the soil. Adult beetles chew leaves at night but are not highly destructive.

Economic Importance: Can cause reduced plant production and even plant loss. Damaging to lawns. Grubs are rarely a problem for organically maintained gardens with healthy, biologically alive soil.

Natural Control: Grow nectar and pollen plants to attract native predators and parasites. Beneficial nematodes.

Organic Control: Beneficial nematodes, compost. Milky spore disease works on Japanese beetle grubs. *Heterorhabditis* nematodes seem to be the most effective nematodes for controlling most destructive grubworms.

Mole Crickets—1"–1¼" brown crickets, larger and uglier than regular crickets

Feeding Habits: Feed on soil insects. Some species eat grass roots.

Economic Importance: Their tunneling damages Bermudagrasses, ornamentals, and vegetables. In some cases, the damage is enough to cause the grass to die.

Natural Control: Insectivorous animals and beneficial nematodes.

Organic Control: Beneficial nematodes applied in the spring. Frequent thin applications of compost or sprayings of compost tea.

Nematodes—unsegmented microscopic worms

Feeding Habits: Troublesome nematodes sometimes feed on grasses. Feeding causes lesions and galls on roots and stimulates excessive branching. Beneficial nematodes feed on grubs, roaches, and termites.

Economic Importance: Plant-attacking nematodes reduce plant vigor, stunt growth, and cause death. Beneficial nematodes provide important control of grubs, roaches, termites, fleas, ticks, and other troublesome pests.

Natural Control: Harmful nematodes are controlled primarily through healthy, biodiverse soil containing beneficial fungi.

Scale Insects—look like cigarette ashes stuck to foliage

Feeding Habits: Scales suck plant sap through piercing, sucking mouthparts. Rarely attack the leaf stems of grasses.

Economic Importance: Can do severe damage by stressing plants and reducing their vigor. Serious citrus pest.

Natural Control: Twice-stabbed, lindorus, and vedalia lady beetles; parasitic aphids; parasitic wasps; healthy plants.

Organic Control: Dormant oil in winter, horticultural oil year-round, and citrus-oil products in the growing season. I personally use orange and Bio-Wash spray.

Sod Webworms—worms that live in small tunnels of silk, usually in a thatch layer

Feeding Habits: At night they feed on the base of the grass plants. Look for leaves cut off at the base. Also look for bare areas around small holes in golf greens and other low-cut turf.

Economic Importance: Intense feeding can damage a lawn seriously.

Natural Control: Protect the wasps, the birds, and the assassin bugs because they eat webworms.

Organic Control: Release trichogramma wasps in the spring. Spray *Bacillus thuringiensis* products, always at dusk, as a last resort. Use one tablespoon of molasses per gallon of spray.

Spiders—long-legged arachnids

Feeding Habits: Paralyze with venom and feed on insects and other small animals.

Economic Importance: Spiders are highly beneficial because they feed on many troublesome insects. Black widows and brown recluses are the only poisonous spiders, and they are very dangerous ones.

Natural Control: Mud daubers and other wasps.

Organic Control: If they have to be killed, use soapy water or an orange product. Eliminate other insects, which are the spiders' food source. All but the black widows and brown recluses are totally beneficial.

Ticks

Feeding Habits: Suck blood of warm-blooded animals.

Economic Importance: Vectors of several diseases.

Natural Control: Cut brush and weeds. Wear protective clothing. Keep interiors well cleaned and vacuumed, fill cracks with steel wool or copper mesh. Ticks have few natural enemies other than fire ants.

Organic Control: Dust with diatomaceous earth for severe infestations. Keep out mice. Stock firewood away from the house. Locate bird feeders away from the house. Spray with citrus oil or d-limonene products. Apply beneficial nematodes.

Disease Control

Diseases are primarily microorganisms that are out of balance. Reestablishing the balance is the key to control. Toxic chemical pesticides not only don't do that, they make the situation worse by killing the beneficial microorganisms. The terms *germs, bacteria,* and *fungi* conjure up negative thoughts, but this should be the case only if they are out of balance.

Plant diseases are usually caused by four major types of living organisms: fungi, bacteria, viruses, and pathogenic nematodes. Diseases are an imbalance of microorganisms and sometimes hard to identify, since the results of infection are more visible than the organisms themselves.

All organic products help control disease. When soil is healthy, there is a never-ending microscopic war being waged between the good and bad microorganisms, and the good guys usually win. Disease problems are simply situations where the microorganisms have gotten out of balance. If allowed to do so, the good guys will control the bad guys. When pathogens are brought into their proper proportions, they are no longer troublesome. In most cases, they become beneficial at that point. Proper drainage is a key ingredient for the prevention of diseases.

As with insects, spraying for diseases is only treating the symptoms, not solving the major problem. The real problem is usually related to the soil and the root system. Therefore it is critical to improve drainage, increase air circulation, add organic material, and stimulate and protect the living organisms in the soil.

Serious lawn diseases are fairly rare. Only during periods of high humidity does the potential for a disease problem exist. The high humidity needed for the development of most diseases can be produced when the lawn is watered too frequently.

Many times a change in the weather or a reduction in watering frequency can "cure" a lawn disease. In other words, drying out a lawn can stop a disease. The exception is St. Augustine Decline (SAD). Choosing a SAD-resistant variety of St. Augustine is desirable.

Here are some of the most common lawn diseases.

BROWN PATCH

This is a cool-weather fungal disease of St. Augustine, although it can be a problem on Bermudagrass. Brown leaves pull loose easily from the runners. Small spots in the lawn grow into large circles or free forms that look bad and weaken the turf but rarely kill the grass. Potassium bicarbonate is a curative spray; soil health, drainage, and low nitrogen input are the best preventatives. Mostly present in spring and fall during periods of frequent rain and high humidity. It is not uncommon for areas that have had brown patch during the previous fall to be the victims of winterkill. Whole ground cornmeal applied at 20 pounds per 1,000 square feet is one of the best solutions. Controls include cornmeal, potassium bicarbonate, Bio-Wash, Serenade, and compost.

DOLLAR SPOT

Fungal disease that attacks most turfgrasses grown in the South. It spreads by water, mowers, other equipment, or shoes. It appears as brown- to straw-colored round and somewhat sunken spots approximately the size of a silver dollar. In coarse-textured grasses, the dead spots are larger. Under these conditions, dollar spot can be confused with brown patch. Control is easy with corn gluten meal or whole ground cornmeal.

GRAY LEAF SPOT

This is another disease that can infect St. Augustine. It's much like helminthosporium in that the infected spot on the leaf is surrounded by a dark margin. Here again, a few spots won't necessarily do any harm, but a lot will. Controls include potassium bicarbonate, baking soda, Serenade, Bio-Wash, and compost.

HELMINTHOSPORIUM

This is a fairly common leaf-spot disease, usually found on Bermudagrass, tall fescue, and ryegrass. The small spots on the leaf blade are brown in the middle with a dark ring. One or two of these infections on a plant's leaf will not seriously hurt it, but as more develop, the leaf's ability to produce food is reduced and the plant becomes weaker. A lawn with a serious infection will slowly thin out. This disease also has been called "fading out" or "thinning out." Controls include cornmeal, potassium bicarbonate, Bio-Wash, Serenade, and compost.

Nigrospora

This is a disease primarily of St. Augustine that affects the stolons or runners. A small lesion develops that looks much like the leaf-spot diseases. The spot grows larger and larger until it completely encircles the runner. This results in the death of all the new plants between the lesion and the end of the runner. It can be promoted by overwatering. Controls include cornmeal, potassium bicarbonate, Bio-Wash, Serenade, and compost.

Pythium

This fungal disease of both perennial ryegrass and Bermudagrass can develop under warm and very wet conditions, especially in low areas of the lawn. The grass takes on a wilted, greasy look at first. Later some spots may have a cottony appearance, and for this reason, the disease may be called cottony blight. The spots may be small circles or they may be streaked. Overwatering may be one of the reasons this disease develops. Controls include cornmeal, potassium bicarbonate, Bio-Wash, Serenade, and compost.

Rust

This is a disease that can be found on most turfgrasses, although zoysia may be the most severely affected. The rust develops orange or brown pustules on the leaves. If you get enough of these on a leaf, the plant's ability to manufacture food is reduced and the turf thins out. Controls include cornmeal, potassium bicarbonate, Bio-Wash, Serenade, and compost.

Slime Mold

This is a turf fungal disease that is mostly cosmetic. Slime mold spore masses coat the grass and look like cigarette ash on the surface of the blades. The spores can easily be wiped off. Remove the mold spores from the grass by rinsing with water during dry weather or mowing and raking at any time. Baking-soda spray or potassium bicarbonate will kill it. So will cornmeal. These molds can cover the aboveground parts of the plant with a dusty dark-gray mass. While slime molds are not too common, it is not uncommon to find them growing on Bermudagrass seed heads. There is no chemical control, and they usually disappear when the weather becomes drier. They tend to develop during wetter weather.

Spring Dead Spot

These are simply circular spots of Bermudagrass that do not green up in the spring. The grass in these spots died sometime during the winter. The organisms that cause this problem have never been identified. The turfgrass will be slow to spread back into these areas. It may take all of the next summer for the dead spots to fill in completely. Usually, seeds will not germinate in these areas for a year or so. Lawns that get spring dead spots usually have been on very high fertility programs, especially those programs that are high in nitrogen.

St. Augustine Decline (SAD)

This is a virus in common St. Augustinegrass that causes a yellow mottling. The grass slowly dies away. The answer is to replace turf with a healthier grass and to plant a mix of native grass, wildflowers, and herbs. This is a serious viral disease of St. Augustine. There is no cure. The lawn will more than likely go through a long, steady decline as more and more plants are infected. A good management program will prolong the life of the affected lawn, but the end is inevitable. It has been said that the only realistic way to deal with St. Augustine Decline is to begin to introduce SAD-resistant varieties into the lawn. Those that have demonstrated resistance are 'Floratam', 'Seville', 'Raleigh', and 'Delmar'. On the other hand, the Basic Organic Program has shown evidence of being able to cure this disease.

Take-All Patch (Bermuda Decline)

This disease can attack several species of grass. It is caused by the fungus *Gaeumannomyces graminis* var. *graminis* and is mostly found in St. Augustinegrass but can also cause problems in Bermudagrass. It is most active during the fall, winter, and spring, especially during moist weather. The first symptom is often yellow leaves and dark roots. The area of discolored and dying leaves will be circular to irregular in shape and up to 20 feet in diameter, and thinning will occur. Unlike with brown patch, the leaves of take-all–infected plants do not easily separate from the plant when pulled. Stolons will often have discolored areas with brown to black roots. Regrowth of the grass into the affected area is often slow and unsuccessful because the new growth becomes infected. Controlling take-all patch is said to be difficult, but it isn't with organic techniques. Good surface and subsurface drainage is important. Cut back on watering and fertilizing. Use only organic fertilizers. If soil compaction exists, aeration will help to alleviate this condition and allow the grass to establish a deeper, more vigorous root system. Prevent take-all patch by maintaining healthy soil. Control the active disease by aeration, applying cornmeal and compost, and using the Basic Organic Program. There are those who recommend applying peat moss for the control of this disease. Peat moss is too expensive and won't work as well as compost used the same way. Stimulating beneficial life in the soil is the key. Peat moss will not do that. It is basically a sterile product, whereas compost is very

Roundup—one of the most fraudulently marketed products ever. It is highly destructive to life in the soil, and its danger to animals and humans is being documented on a regular basis now.

much alive. If lowering the pH is the aim, it can be accomplished much more cheaply and efficiently with vinegar.

Weed Control

Weeds or so-called weeds are way overblown. Weeding is an ongoing process, but it is not difficult once you establish a healthy lawn. Healthy grass is extremely competitive and will itself crowd out most weeds. If a lot of weeds do pop up, it is a sign that your grass is in stress. This could mean your soil is deficient or waterlogged, or it could mean you're cutting the grass too short. Weeds will also pop up in a healthy lawn of course. For the most part, this isn't anything to worry about. Almost all lawns have weeds, and they don't do much harm in small numbers. Simply pull up any weeds that detract from the lawn's appearance. If you have a larger weed problem, spray the individual weeds with a low-toxicity herbicide. Don't spray the entire lawn unless you have weeds throughout. Late-winter or early-spring weeds is one of the most common issues homeowners in the South deal with, and it has an easy solution. The entire lawn can be sprayed between Thanksgiving and Christmas with a vinegar-based herbicide, which will kill the young weeds without harming the dormant summer grasses.

The year I was born, the Scotts Company introduced its "weed-and-feed" product that unfortunately is still on the market. Hopefully this product and its herbicide, atrazine, will be gone before the first printing of this book.

> The killing of weeds is big business.

The most serious and perhaps the most frustrating pest problem associated with a lawn is that of weeds. No lawn is immune to them. Weeds are the opportunists of the plant world. A weed is ready to take advantage of any failure in the lawn's maintenance, or at least it seems that way. In considering weed controls, there are a couple of facts you should know. First, weed seed is all over the place, in virtually every soil; second, weed seed can live in the soil for years and years just waiting for a chance to germinate. The primary control of weeds is to eliminate the conditions in which the weeds are able to germinate and grow.

In developing a weed control program, there is absolutely no question that the front line in the "Weed War" is the adherence to a good lawn maintenance program that produces a thick, dense turf. Weeds rarely invade a high-quality lawn. All the money in the world can be spent on weed-controlling chemicals, but if the lawn is not maintained properly, chances are the weeds will return.

Once a weed is in place, it must be removed either mechanically by digging or chemically. If the choice is by digging, all the underground parts of the weed that are capable of growing a new plant, such as the rhizome, must be removed. Rhizomes may extend undetected from above the soil to several inches or even a foot beyond the base of the weed. If not completely removed, the weed will reestablish itself in a short period of time. Generally, perennial weeds have underground parts like rhizomes, while annual weeds do not.

When considering chemical control, it should be remembered that a chemical that is toxic to plants is being used to remove an undesirable plant (the weed) from a population of desirable plants (the lawn). Sometimes this is difficult. An example of this process is the fact that it takes more MSMA to kill common Bermudagrass than it does to kill crabgrass, so if the proper rates of MSMA are used, the crabgrass will die and the worst that happens to the Bermuda is that it gets a little yellow for a while. Chemical proponents use this ridiculous argument to try to justify their chemicals. MSMA is an arsenic compound! Luckily for everyone, it has now been taken off the market, even though the organiphobes are still lamenting its demise.

Sometimes, weeds are very hard to control even though the right chemical is applied properly. Basically, the chemical, which can kill the weed, must enter the plant either through tiny openings in the leaves or through the root system. If it is a hot and dry day, these leaf openings may be closed, and if soil moisture levels are low, the root system might not take up the chemical. The rule of thumb is that the weed must be actively growing for it to be controlled. A cooler day a few days after a good rain might be a prime time for weed control. A lot of weed-control failures can be traced to unfavorable weather conditions. Also, the younger a weed is, the easier it is to control. Old weeds can be very tough. This is good advice for the use of the toxic chemicals as well as the use of the sensible organic products like vinegar.

There are thousands of plants that one time or another could or have been called weeds. Weeds can be both annual and perennial plants. They are either grasslike in their appearance or they are called a broadleaf weed.

Commonly available weed-control products may be divided into two large groups: those that kill the weed seed as it germinates (called preemergent herbicides), and those that control the weed after it germinates (postemergent herbicides).

Preemergent Weed Control

With preemergent weed controls, a chemical is applied evenly over the lawn and forms a barrier at the soil surface. The theory is that no germinating seed, be it weed or even grass seed, can penetrate this barrier without being killed. If not disturbed, the barrier can remain in place from a few months up to or over a year. The type of soil and the amount of water used on the lawn has a lot to do with the life of the barrier.

The biggest problem with the use of preemergent herbicides is that of timing. The chemical must be in place before the weed seed begins to grow, and the beginning of weed growth usually is tied to weather patterns. A whole host of annuals, like henbit and annual bluegrass, germinate in the fall as soon as the weather cools off. There could be as much as a month or so difference in the arrival of the first significant cold front.

The same situation is present in the spring. Many annuals, like knotweed and crabgrass, germinate in early spring, again depending on temperatures. In northern Texas, for example, the preemergent herbicide should be applied by March 1 and, of course, even earlier farther south. But there are years when these dates may be too late. The success of a good preemergent program, aside from considerations like using the proper rate and obtaining an even distribution, depends on changes in the weather. Early or late falls and early or late springs make preemergent programs difficult. All that can be done is to follow the averages and accept the fact that once in a while the program may fail. It's interesting that the same timing concerns apply to the toxic chemical and the organic choice, corn gluten meal.

Postemergent Weed Control

Postemergent chemicals are used to control weeds after they come up. Weeds, for control purposes, are divided into two groups—those that are grassy in appearance and the broadleaf types. When selecting a postemergent product, care must be given to make sure the product will control the weed without harming the lawn or any ornamental plants in or near the lawn. The postemergent organic products include vinegar, citrus products, fatty-acid products, and essential-oil products.

Grassy Weed Control

These are the hardest of the weeds to control because there just aren't many products available that can selectively remove a grassy weed from among the desirable turfgrass plants. Many chemicals have the potential of killing any of the turfgrasses. Removing the weedy grasses such as crabgrass, goosegrass, and Johnsongrass without harming the desirable turfgrasses may be a matter of concentration. A weaker solution may kill the weedy grass, while a more concentrated form of the same chemical could kill the desirable turfgrass. It is critical that the label on the chemical's container be read and understood. Be sure it is safe to use on the turfgrass variety in the lawn and that the grassy weed targeted for removal is listed on the label. Again, the application rates may be critical. Crabgrass is rarely a problem in healthy, organically maintained turf.

Broadleaf Weed Control

Several products are sold for controlling broadleaf weeds in any lawn. These products are usually mixtures of several chemicals. Listed on each of the containers is a list of the broadleaf weeds, the formulation controls, and which of the turfgrasses won't be harmed. Also, look for any warning concerning the use of the chemical around ornamental plants. Unfortunately, most of the products in this category are toxic chemicals and not recommended.

Annual Bluegrass (*Poa annua*)

This small cool-season grass is a particularly serious weed problem in closely mowed areas. It begins to emerge in late summer and early fall when night temperatures are in the sixties and moisture is present. Annual bluegrass seeds continue to germinate through the fall, winter, and spring, making control more difficult. Favored by moist soil conditions and cool temperatures. It has a strong competitive advantage over warm-season grasses from fall through spring. Annual bluegrass is greatly reduced by taller mowing heights and limited use of water. Seed heads form in late fall and winter, but seed-head development is greatest in the spring and early summer. Controlled with preemergent herbicides like corn gluten meal and postemergent herbicides like vinegar.

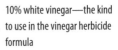

10% white vinegar—the kind to use in the vinegar herbicide formula

Black Medic (*Medicago lupulina*)

Black medic is an annual or sometimes a perennial. Stems are hairy and branch at the base. Branches are prostrate and spreading. Flowers are small and yellow in short, round heads.

Burclover (*Medicago polymorpha*)

Burclover is a perennial that is very similar in appearance to black medic. It contains three oblong leaflets, with the center leaflet being on its own petiole. The leaflets often have brown spots on the upper surface. The flowers of burclover are yellow. Burclover reproduces by seeds from "burred" seed pods as well as spreading prostrate stolons, which allows burclover to tolerate close mowing. Burclover is found from Virginia south to Florida and west to Texas and Missouri. This plant is a clear indicator of lousy soil and poor fertility.

Common Chickweed (*Stellaria media*)

Common chickweed is a winter annual that is a low-growing succulent weed that often spreads out in extensive mats. It may survive summer in moist, shady, cool areas. Seed leaves have prominent midveins and are about four times as long as they are broad, tapering to a point at the tip. True leaves are broader, opposite, and yellow green. Flowers are small but showy with five deeply cut white petals. Several plants have been named chickweed, one of them a plant belonging to the Purslane family and four species of Cerastium, the mouse-ear chickweeds. Young leaves when boiled can hardly be distinguished from spring spinach and are equally wholesome. They may also be used uncooked with young dandelion leaves to form a salad.

Clover, White (*Trifolium repens*)

Perennial. Round flower heads consisting of twenty to forty white to pinkish-white florets on long stems. Creeping stems up to 15 inches long with dark-green three-part leaves. Roots occur at the joints of the stems. Deeply rooted, it likes cool weather and clay soils. Evergreen when irrigated in the summer. Plant in September or October for best results. Ground cover, cover crop, turf plant. One of the nation's most important pasture legumes. Great for soil building because of its deep roots and nitrogen-fixing ability. Usually considered a weed, but it shouldn't be. I encourage it in my lawn.

Crabgrass (*Digitaria sanguinalis*)

Crabgrass is the major annual weed infesting home lawns. It germinates in April, sets seed in August, and dies with the first frost of fall. Crabgrass has tremendous survival reproductive capabilities. A few crabgrass plants in your lawn are acceptable. The most effective way to control crabgrass is to create a dense, healthy turf. Preemergent herbicides prevent the emergence of crabgrass plants. These products must be applied prior to crabgrass germination, which could occur as early as April 1. Postemergent herbicides control crabgrass after it has emerged. These products are most effective on small crabgrass. Do not attempt to control crabgrass after about July 15, because it is too large to control effectively. It is better to simply tolerate it until it dies with the first frost. However, it can be killed by spraying the vinegar-based herbicides.

Dallisgrass (*Paspalum dilatatum*)

This warm-season perennial is one of the most troublesome weeds in lawns. It begins growth in very early spring and prefers warm, moist areas and high-cut lawns. Tolerates almost any type of soil, reproducing by seeds and rhizomes (underground stems). It has long, coarse-textured leaves ½ inch wide and 4–10 inches long. Stems 2–6 inches long radiate from the center of the plant in a star pattern. Seeds are produced on three to five finger-like seg-

Dallisgrass—common and difficult weed to control in summer

ments that grow from the top of these stems from May to October. Seed stalks grow tall and are unattractive in lawns. Plants form slightly spreading clumps with deep roots. It grows most vigorously in warm summer weather but can remain green in mild winters. Control with vinegar-based herbicides and physical removal.

Dandelion (*Taraxacum officinale*)
Perennial. Yellow flowers and powder-puff seed heads, lettuce-like foliage, deep tap root. Flowers are used in cookies and wine, young foliage in salads, the root in tea. The aggressive root system brings minerals from the subsoil up to the surface. Considered a lawn weed. Aeration and proper use of organic fertilizers will greatly reduce the population. Easy to kill if necessary by spraying with full-strength vinegar or removing manually.

Dichondra (*Dichondra micrantha*)
Perennial lawn plant or ground cover. Very low growing, spreads by runners. Tiny lily-pad-looking leaves. Likes partial to heavy shade and moist soil. Excellent between stepping stones. Sometimes used as turf. Many people don't understand that dichondra is a beautiful ground cover instead of a noxious weed to be sprayed with toxic herbicides. Can be killed with broadleaf herbicides, but why? If you don't like it, let the soil dry out more between waterings. Sometimes sold as *Dichondra carolinensis* or *Dichondra repens*.

Dandelion—a weed that is an edible herb

Dollarweed (*Hydrocotyle* spp.)

Also known as pennywort, this is a warm-season perennial weed. The common
name comes from its shiny silver dollar–shaped leaves. The leaves are round,
bright green, and fleshy and look like miniature lily pads measuring 1–2
inches in diameter with scalloped edges. It has a low-growing habit that
spreads by seeds, rhizomes, and tubers. It is often confused with dichondra.
To distinguish between the two, look at the placement of the leaf stem. Dollarweed has a stem located in the center of the leaf, while dichondra's stem
is located at the edge. Dichondra's leaves are also smaller and lower growing. This is not an easy-to-control weed. In the past I have said all you can
do is dry out the area and hand-pull the weed. However, here's an idea that
is worth a try. Use the Garden Weasel Crabgrass Killer. Since this product
works best on rough-textured leaves, spray the dollarweed first with Bio-
Wash or diluted vinegar.

Fairy Ring—Toadstool, Mushroom

Fruiting bodies of fungi growing on decaying organic matter. It has white caps
that look like golf balls when young; they expand to 4–8 inches in diameter
at maturity. Usually appear in lawns in summer after rainy periods. Caps are
white at first, then turn gray green and have distinctive green spores, reddish-
brown "scales" on the cap, and a ring on the smooth stalk. Fairy rings usually

grow in soil where wood is decaying, such as roots or an old stump. Very toxic! Known for their tendency to collect heavy metals from the air and soil.

Goosegrass (*Eleusine indica*)

Goosegrass, also called wiregrass, is an annual weed that grows as a compressed plant in turf. It appears as a silvery mat forming a pale-green clump with a low rosette and flattened stems. Flower stalks are short, stout, and compressed. Seed heads are somewhat similar to those of Dallisgrass but short and stiff. Normally found in compacted areas or areas of heavy wear. Produces seed even under close mowing. Control with healthy soil and spraying vinegar-based products. Common on golf greens in the South.

Grassbur (*Cenchrus echinatus*)

Field sandbur (grassbur) is a summer annual grassy weed adapted to dry, sandy soils, but it can be found growing in other types of soils as well. Sharp, spiny burs generally start germinating in late spring and will continue to germinate until late summer or early fall months. It will continue to grow until the first hard frost or freeze occurs in the fall. Generally not a problem in well-maintained turfgrass areas. The most effective and efficient method of control is to use a preemergent herbicide.

Henbit (*Lamium amplexicaule*)

This is a winter annual that reproduces by seed and rooting stems. Henbit stems droop and then turn upright to grow to 16 inches tall. They may root where they touch the ground. They are square, green to purplish, and smooth or hairy. The roots are fibrous. Leaves are ½ to 1 inch long. Henbit flowers are tubular, pink to red to purple. Henbit is often found growing in moist, fertile soils. To control henbit without herbicides, maintain density and health in established turf and remove seedlings in the autumn. Small populations can be hoed or hand-pulled or sprayed with vinegar-based organic herbicides. Preemergent herbicides (corn gluten meal) should be applied in late summer before germination.

Johnsongrass (*Sorghum halepense*)

One of the most troublesome of perennial grasses. It reproduces from underground stems and seeds. Grows in spreading, leafy patches that may be as tall as 6 to 7 feet. Leaves have a prominent whitish midvein, which snaps readily when folded over. The flower head is large, open, well branched, and often reddish tinged. Underground stems are thick, fleshy, and segmented. Roots and shoots can rise from each segment. Control by mowing—it can't stand the pressure.

Nutgrass/Nutsedge (*Cyperus esculentus*)

Nutsedge, also called purple or yellow nutgrass, is a perennial pest in lawns and gardens. The erect, single, triangular stem has narrow, grasslike, yellow-green leaves. Leaves point outward in three directions. Blooms in late summer to early fall. Seed heads are yellow brown. Plant tops die back in the fall, leaving underground tubers to overwinter in the soil and repeat the cycle the following year. Nutgrass reproduces by seeds as well as tubers, which are generally the size of popcorn kernels. Weeds sprout in late spring and early summer. A single tuber of yellow nutsedge is capable of producing 146 tubers within fourteen weeks following planting and can infest an area 6½ feet in diameter. It is a difficult weed to control, but several reports have come in that heavy amounts of molasses drenched in infested areas kill out the plants over several months. This is a sedge and likes moist, anaerobic soils, so changing that condition is the best approach. Applying hydrogen peroxide and generally improving the drainage both help. Use 3 percent hydrogen peroxide at about 16 ounces per gallon of water and drench problem areas.

Purslane (*Portulaca oleracea*)

Common purslane is a low-growing annual that grows rapidly in spring and summer. It thrives under dry conditions but also competes well in irrigated situations. Leaves are very succulent and often tinged red. Small yellow flowers are borne singly or in clusters of two or three. Flowers usually open only on sunny mornings. Purslane seeds are very tiny and produced in abundance. The entire plant is edible and nutritious. It is easy to kill with vinegar and other organic herbicides, but remember that it is a tasty and healthful herb and vegetable for cooking or used raw in salads.

Rescuegrass (*Bromus catharticus*)

This is a common cool-season weed that shows up dramatically in the late winter and early spring in warm-season turf areas where the grass has not yet greened up. It is an annual or perennial grass growing up to 3 feet in height if not mowed. It can be sprayed and killed easily with vinegar or d-limonene products while the seedlings are still small. Once the plants are large, several sprayings are usually needed.

Roadside Aster (*Aster exilis*)

This is an annual that has a small white flower in late spring. Usually is found growing in fairly poor soils. It will not compete with turfgrasses if the lawn is healthy. It is an easy-to-control weed/wildflower by increasing the vigor of the lawn with organic soil amendments and fertilizers.

Spurge (*Euphorbia maculata*)

Spotted spurge grows close to the ground, often forming a dense mat. Its green leaves, which grow in pairs, are ⅛ to ½ inch long and about ⅛ inch wide. Frequently a red spot will mark the leaf halfway down its center vein. Flowers, fruit, stems, and leaves are hairy. Broken stems and branches secrete a milky, poisonous sap. Although spotted spurge sap is being studied as a cure for various skin cancers, in general, the sap of all members of this genus is an eye and skin irritant.

It has tiny, pinkish flowers. The fruit is a three-celled seed capsule. The plant's central taproot system is capable of extending more than 24 inches into the soil. It is easy to remove by hand and easy to kill with the vinegar or d-limonene herbicides.

CHAPTER 5

Products for Lawn Care

Amendments/Fertilizers

*A*ctivated Sludge: Activated sludge is produced when sewage is aerated by air bubbled rapidly through it. Certain types of active bacteria coagulate the organic matter that settles out, leaving a clear liquid that can be discharged or used for irrigation. Activated sludge is generally heat and/or microbe treated and dried before being sold. It is the method used to produce Milorganite or Hou-Actinite. These companies do an excellent job keeping the heavy metals and pathogens from being problems, but pharmaceuticals are still a concern.

Alfalfa Meal: Alfalfa provides many nutritional benefits not only for plant use but for soil organisms as well. One very important ingredient is tricontanol, a powerful plant growth regulator. Orchid and rose growers make an alfalfa tea and spray it directly as a foliar fertilizer. Alfalfa is very high in vitamins, plus N-P-K-Ca, Mg, and other valuable minerals. It also includes sugars, starches, proteins, fiber, and sixteen amino acids.

Alfalfa Tea: Put one cup alfalfa meal per 5 gallons of water. Stir and let the mixture sit from one to four days. The result will be a thick tea. Apply generously to the root area of shrubs and flowers or use as a foliar spray after straining the solids out. The longer it brews, the better it is but the worse it will smell.

Azomite: Azomite is an acronym for the "A to Z of minerals, including trace elements." It was created 30 million years ago by a volcanic eruption that filled a nearby seabed. The unique combination of seawater fed by rivers rich in minerals and rare earth elements present in the volcanic ash created this mineral composition deposit. This is an excellent rock mineral product that works well with carbon material such as compost and organic fertilizers to create a complete soil feeding program. It can be used at 20–100 pounds per square feet.

Basalt: Available in many forms, such as sand, crushed, or weathered. It is an igneous rock formed from molten lava that is low in oxygen but rich in iron and magnesium. It is also paramagnetic, although values vary according to exact type. Basalt improves all soil properties.

Blood Meal: Smelly source of nitrogen and phosphorus sometimes used mixed with cottonseed meal. Expensive, but it's good to use occasionally. Analysis can range from 12-2-1 to 11-0-0. This natural meal has a low pH and many trace minerals, including iron. Use at 20 pounds per 1,000 square feet or 300–400 pounds per acre. A good blend is made by mixing 80 percent cottonseed meal with 20 percent blood meal. If zeolite is blended in with these two products, it helps reduce odor and makes them last a lot longer. Blend in at the rate of 1–3 percent.

Bone Meal: Slow-release source of calcium and phosphorus recommended for bulbs, tomatoes, and other vegetables. Analysis will range from 2-12-0 to 4-12-0 with 2 to 5 percent calcium. Slower acting and more expensive than soft rock phosphate. Young bones usually have less phosphorus and more nitrogen than older bones. Commonly available steamed bone meal is made from bones that have been boiled or steamed at high pressure to remove fats and proteins. This process reduces nitrogen but increases phosphorus. Bone meal works more quickly on well-aerated soil. Not highly recommended.

Bottom Ash: Produced from the burning of coal but often contains lead, arsenic, mercury, cadmium, and other toxic materials that become concentrated in the ash. It is not recommended for use in horticulture, agriculture, or anything else, as it's too toxic.

Chelators: Chelated iron and other chelated nutrients are used when a direct dose of a particular nutrient is needed to quickly solve a deficiency. Chelated products are organic compounds with attached inorganic metal molecules, which are more available for plant use. Compost, humus, humic acid, and microorganisms have natural chelating properties.

Chicken Manure: Chicken litter is a good natural fertilizer high in nitrogen. Pelletized forms are better because they are not as dusty. Approximate analysis is 6-4-2. Unfortunately, commercial chickens are still being fed lots of unnatural things, including arsenic. It's always best to compost manure products before using them. When used, apply at 25 pounds per 1,000 square feet or 400 pounds per acre. Pathogens and heavy metals are a concern, but most companies monitor and keep these materials from being in the products at problem levels. The larger concern relates to pharmaceuticals, which are also a worry for feedlot manures and human sewer products. No one has figured out how to get these dangerous drugs out of the products.

Chilean Nitrate: Fast-acting source of nitrogen, 16 percent nitrogen that is almost immediately available. Sodium nitrate or Chilean saltpeter, which is impure natural sodium nitrate, is not an acceptable natural organic fertilizer and should never be used on soil with salt problems. It is too fast acting and too harsh. Fertilizers containing this product should not be used.

Coffee Grounds: Approximate analysis is 2-3-6. An excellent natural fertilizer with an acid pH and up to 2 percent nitrogen. Collect grounds at home and from your local restaurant or coffee shop and use in the compost pile or apply directly to the soil at 20–80 pounds per 1,000 square feet. Coffee grounds are a natural soil amendment and acid organic matter for bed preparation. Use directly in alkaline soils or mix into the compost pile.

Coir: Shredded fiber from coconut husks. Slow to decompose, helps loosen and aerate soils, used in potting mixes, is a renewable resource. Contains N-P-K and trace minerals and is an excellent product for stimulating biological activity in the soil. Often woven into mats and used to line hanging baskets. This could be useful in seedbed preparation but is more commonly used in potting soils.

Colloidal Rock Phosphate (same as soft rock phosphate): A mixture of fine particles of phosphate suspended in a clay base. An economical form of natural phosphorus and calcium. Unlike chemically made phosphates, rock phosphate is insoluble in water, will not leach away, and therefore is long lasting. It has 18 percent phosphorus and 15 percent calcium as well as trace elements. Florida is the primary source.

Copper Sulfate: Ingredient used in algaecides and fungicides. Also called bluestone, it has been used to control root growth in sewer pipes and storm drains. Also used for algae control in ponds. It has also been recommended as a copper trace mineral source for fertilizer use. This product has been banned in some states for use in water and should be banned everywhere. Its overuse causes severe toxicity. At best, it only offers a short-term control of pond algae. It is used in highly diluted concentrations on plants for control of black spots on roses. I do not recommend the use of this product.

Corn Gluten Meal: Corn gluten meal is a natural preemergent fertilizer (9.5-0.5-0.5) that reduces the germination and establishment of troublesome annual weeds. It is available as a powder or in granular form. It is 60 percent protein and approximately 10 percent nitrogen by weight. It is a by-product of the wet milling process and commonly used in pet and livestock feed. It can be used in vegetable gardens as a fertilizer and can help with weed control, but be careful, as it can damage the germination of your food crops. Use it only after your vegetable seeds are up and young plant roots are well established. It is a powerful fertilizer and will create large healthy weeds if applied after they germinate. This unique use of corn gluten meal was discovered by Dr. Nick Christians and his research staff at Iowa State University. Corn gluten meal is on the market as an EPA-registered product. It's available in bags at most local nurseries and feed stores specializing in organic products. It was determined that corn gluten meal stops root formation of germinating sprouts. Seeds treated with corn gluten meal developed top shoots but no roots and died when water was withheld from the soil surface. It was also tested for detrimental effects on established grasses. Not only does corn gluten meal not damage mature grass, it is an excellent natural organic fertilizer. However, it has lost favor in the organic industry in the last few years. For one thing, it is too expensive. The cost has risen because of corn sales to make ethanol and because China buys it as a protein source. The other issue is that it is less than effective in many years, especially in the fall. It's a reasonable tool to use in an organic program but possibly not worth the cost.

Cornmeal: Cornmeal is a powerful natural fungus control. It may also be effective on other soil-borne diseases. Apply to soil at 10–20 pounds per 1,000 square feet. Use at 20 pounds per 1,000 square feet or 200–800 pounds per acre to add cellulose and stimulate the beneficial microorganisms that control several disease pathogens such as Rhizoctonia, Pythium, Fusarium, Phytophthora, and others. Can also be used in pools and water features to control algae at 2 cups of cornmeal per 100 square feet or 150 pounds per acre. It is also useful on pond algae. Apply to ponds and lakes at 150–200 pounds per acre to control algae.

Cotton Boll Compost (Cotton bur compost): Compost made from cotton-processing waste. It has an approximate analysis of 7-2-2, an acid pH, and lots of trace minerals. It has possible pesticide residue because so many toxic poisons are used in the cotton industry. Use at 20–25 pounds per 1,000 square feet or 700–800 pounds per acre.

Cottonseed Meal: Natural organic fertilizer with an acid pH. Good natural source of nitrogen and trace elements. Cottonseed meal is made from the cotton seed. A special value of cottonseed meal is its acid pH, which makes it a valuable fertilizer for acid-loving specialty crops. Analysis will vary and ranges from 6-2-1 to 7-3-2 with trace elements. It does have an odor for a while after use.

Diatomaceous Earth (DE): Used as a source of silicon. Occurs naturally and in a calcined form is used in filter media. Raw DE has moisture-absorbing powers and is used in insect control. It is also used in animal feeds for internal parasite control and to pull toxins out of the body. The DE used for swimming pools and other filter media is dangerous to breathe and does not have any use in plant or animal management.

Dolomite: Dolomite or dolomitic lime is a type of lime or limestone rich in magnesium. Chemically, it is a mineral called calcium magnesium carbonate. Dolomite is quarried, pulverized, and sold as an agricultural lime powder. Because of the magnesium content, it is not recommended as much as high-calcium lime unless the soil is deficient in calcium and magnesium. High-calcium lime, calcium carbonate, is the recommended treatment for most calcium-deficient soils.

Epsom Salt: Known as magnesium sulfate or Epsom salt ($MgSO_4$), it provides Mg and S and does not alter pH. Small amounts help remove sodium from soils. This is a good source of magnesium and sulfur. Epsom salt is made by treating magnesium hydroxide or magnesium carbonate with sulfuric acid. Magnesium is a vital element in the production of chlorophyll in plants. A deficiency shows in the discoloration of the leaves between the veins, which develops into dead areas if the condition is allowed to persist. Epsom salt is a fast-acting source of magnesium and sulfur normally used as a foliar food, but it can also be applied to soil. Use 1 tablespoon per gallon and spray monthly if needed on flowering plants. Broadcast at the rate of 5–10 pounds per 1,000 square feet. It can also be applied by putting a small amount in transplant holes of vegetables and flowers. Epsom salt is not a natural organic product but is acceptable to organic practitioners.

Expanded Shale: The product known as expanded shale is produced from clay minerals that are found in nature in various forms. Some types of clay, shale (clay that has heat and pressure applied to it to form the shale), and slate (formed by lots of heat and pressure over geologic time) can be used. The clay minerals or rocks are crushed and then fired in an oven at high heat. This process causes the minerals to expand into a rocklike aggregate that is screened into various sizes. These aggregates are lighter than gravel and are very hard, hence they are used to make lightweight concrete. They are frequently used as an ingredient in making soil mixes for green roofs, as they hold their structure and are lighter than soil and sand.

Granite: Available in many forms: sand, crushed, weathered. It is an igneous rock prized by gardeners for its ability to improve plant growth and many soil properties. Granite is composed of oxygen-rich minerals that release many nutrients slowly over time by the action of soil microbes. Granite is also paramagnetic, although values vary according to exact type and source.

Greensand (Glauconite): An iron-potassium silicate that is green in color due to the minerals it contains. Naturally occurring greenish mineral powder with the texture of fine sand. The most common type is found in New Jersey, hence it is called Jersey Greensand. It is a primary source of potassium but also contains iron, magnesium, calcium, phosphorus, and up to thirty other trace minerals necessary for plant health in a mineral-insoluble form. These minerals must be digested by microbes in the soil before becoming available for plants. Greensand is a proven soil conditioner that enriches and mineralizes most soils. It is the most cost-effective source of plant nutrients, often containing up to 12 percent iron. There are deposits in many places around the country. It is one of the few iron supplements I recommend.

Gypsum ($CaSO_4$): Gypsum is a naturally occurring mineral that is made up of calcium sulfate and water ($CaSO_4 + 2H_2O$) that is sometimes called hydrous calcium sulfate. It is the mineral calcium sulfate with two water molecules attached. By weight, it is 79 percent calcium sulfate and 21 percent water. Gypsum has 23 percent calcium and 18 percent sulfur, and its solubility is 150 times that of limestone, thus it is a natural source of plant nutrients. Gypsum naturally occurs in sedimentary deposits from ancient seabeds. Gypsum is mined and made into many products like drywall used in construction, agriculture, and industry. It is also a by-product of many industrial processes. One of the major uses of gypsum is to remove sodium salts from soils.

Humates: Humates are the partially decomposed remains of ancient plants that have been buried and exposed to heat and pressure over geological time frames but not enough to form coal. Excellent source of humic materials that help soils retain nutrients and provide a food source for many beneficial microbes.

Lava Sand: Lava sand is a by-product of mining and crushing lava to make landscape gravel and rocks. Depending on the minerals in the lava, it may be reddish or black. The magma that produced the lava flows often cools relatively quickly in geologic terms, leaving the material paramagnetic. The crushing and screening process often produces very small particles (silt sized to fine sand) that arc called "lava sand." These smaller particles will help coarser soils hold water better and do not decompose over time as would humus or compost, so they permanently change the physical properties of the soil. The beneficial properties of lava sand vary greatly depending on the source.

Leonardite: This is oxidized lignite coal that is composed mainly of humic substances (humic and fulvic acids), which increase the availability of macro and micro nutrients. These substances also promote plant growth and make fertilizers more efficient, hence less is required.

Lime (CaO): Sometimes called quicklime, as it is very reactive chemically, it is produced by heating limestone to high temperatures. Very alkaline and used to make mortar, plaster, cement soil, concrete, and has other uses as well. Not the best choice for horticulture as a calcium source.

Limestone ($CaCO_3$): Used as a natural calcium source and to raise the pH of the soil. The extra calcium reduces the negative effects of aluminum on plant growth. Most limestone contains various amounts of magnesium also in the form of $MgCO_3$. When the magnesium content is over 10 percent of the mineral, then it is called dolomitic lime or dolomite, as it contains both $CaCO_3$ and $MgCO_3$.

Milorganite: Sewer-sludge fertilizer from Milwaukee. Has been widely used on golf courses. Had a scare for a while that the product caused Lou Gehrig's disease, but this was proven to be false. It's best not to use any sewer-sludge product on edible plants. Many cities now make a similar product. This is a very high-quality product, and they do an excellent job keeping the heavy metals and pathogens from being problems, but pharmaceuticals are still a real concern.

Molasses, Dry (Dried Molasses): Dry molasses isn't dried molasses. It's a grain residue carrier, such as bits of soy meal that is sprayed and covered with liquid molasses. It's an excellent carbon source that stimulates beneficial microorganisms. And, it repels fire ants. Apply to soil for landscaping at 20 pounds per 1,000 square feet for ideal results. Farmers and ranchers can use it at much lower rates and still get acceptable results. As little as 100–200 pounds per acre can be beneficial. Apply when the air and ground are dry to avoid creating a sticky mess. It cannot be mixed with water and sprayed.

The sugar level in quality dry molasses should be 42 percent versus the 38 percent and less that is on the market. The Stockade dry-molasses products contain the proper amount of sugar.

Molasses, Liquid: Liquid molasses is a sweet syrup that is used as a food but also as a soil amendment to feed and stimulate microorganisms. It is normally sprayed at 1–2 ounces per gallon of water. Like the dry molasses, it provides food for microorganisms and is a source of carbon, sulfur, and potash. It is a quick source of energy for the soil life and microbes living in the soil or the compost pile, and will help chase fire ants away. Liquid molasses is used in sprays to help organic pest controls and as an ingredient in many organic fertilizers. It is also a major ingredient in liquid Garrett Juice.

Liquid molasses is an excellent foliar-feeding material by itself and can be mixed with other organic liquids. It can be used for agriculture at 2–4 quarts per acre for soil application. For foliar application on broadleaf plants, use 1 pint per acre. For grasses and grains, use 1 quart per acre. Blackstrap molasses is the best choice because it contains the sulfur and iron of the original material. Since it is hard to find, any molasses will work, but in general, the darker ones work best. None of the liquid-molasses products last as long as the dry version.

Mushroom Compost: Planting media in which mushrooms are grown, consisting mainly of peat, straw, gypsum, and animal manure. It is not a composted material. Spent mushroom compost is widely available and is a useful addition to garden soils, since it increases the supply of organic matter and water retention. It tends to be dense and to hold water too long at times. Coarse-textured compost or shredded bark mixed with it helps improve the quality. It's not a good product for organic management.

Peat Moss: Used for many years as a soil amendment and in potting mixes. Its usage is now not recommended, since it is not a renewable resource, as wetlands have to be destroyed to harvest the peat moss. Does not support beneficial microbes or provide nutrients, as would good compost. It is a good product to use for storage of perishable materials such as bulbs for the winter. The reason it works so well is its antimicrobial properties—just the opposite of what the soil needs. Some are now recommending peat moss as an application for control of take-all patch. I think that it is far too expensive and does not work nearly as well as compost.

Perlite: Mined from a silicon-rich volcanic rock that has been heated to 1,800°F. The heating causes it to expand into a lightweight porous sterile media. It has a gritty feel and looks sort of like Styrofoam pellets; it often floats in water. Contains no available nutrients but does help improve drainage and aeration of some soils. Does not break down or deteriorate in the soil. Not a good lawn seedbed improvement product.

Pumice: A volcanic rock formed from ash from volcanoes. It tends to be a very porous, lightweight mineral. It has been used to increase the water-holding capacity of soils. Would be okay to use, but lava sand is much better.

Rabbit Manure: Approximate analysis is from 2-1-5 to 3-2-1. Rabbit manure is not used enough: it is an excellent source of natural nutrition. Mixed with leaves, sawdust, straw, grass, and other vegetative materials, it makes excellent compost. Rabbit manure is rich in nitrogen, is good for heating a compost pile, and can be applied directly to the garden soil. It can be used on lawns, vegetable gardens, and around trees and shrubs all through the year. Sawdust, straw, dry leaves, grass, cedar flakes, and similar dry materials can be used for litter in the hutch, producing an excellent compost when the droppings and urine are caught and absorbed by these materials. Earthworms love rabbit manure. Rabbit-manure compost is an excellent soil builder. Can be used directly as a fertilizer without fear of burning plants. Llama and alpaca manures can also be used directly without composting first.

Sea Minerals: This is a group of products produced from seawater or the ocean. Seawater has over ninety minerals in it, thus products from the ocean often have the same minerals. Some of these products are just sea salt or minerals produced by removing the water. Others are mined products from ancient sea-salt deposits that have been weathered and much of the sodium has been leached out. Two of the best products in this category are Redmond Sea Salt and Redmond Clay.

Seaweed: Best used as a foliar spray. Excellent source of trace minerals. Should be used often. Contains hormones that stimulate root growth and branching. Many trace elements are found in seaweed in the proportions they are found in plants. Seaweed contains hormones and functions as a mild but effective insect control, especially for whiteflies and spider mites. It acts as a chelating agent, making other fertilizers and nutrients more available to the plants. Seaweed or kelp is available in liquid form and in dry meals.

Sugar: Sugar is a helpful soil amendment used to stimulate microorganisms and to initiate the metabolic processes in the soil. White sugar, when used with other trace minerals in natural organic fertilizers, is an excellent carbohydrate source. Molasses is an even better form of sugar. For more on the benefits of sugar, read Dr. Arden Andersen's *Science in Agriculture*. Sugar should be used on gardens or fields at about 5–10 pounds per 1,000 square feet or less. Some farmers are using small amounts per acre of sugar, humate, and urea. A starting formula for transition to an organic program could be 30–50 pounds of sugar, 50–100 pounds of humate, and 50–100 pounds of urea per acre.

Sulfur: Finely ground sulfur is used by mixing with water or dusting on dry plants to control black spot, leaf spot, brown canker, rust, peach leaf curl, powdery mildew, apple scab, and many insect pests. Mix with liquid seaweed to enhance fungicidal properties. Sulfur will also control fleas, mites, thrips, and chiggers. To avoid leaf burn, do not use when temperature is 90 degrees or above. As an insecticide or fungicide, use 3 tablespoons per gallon of water. Sulfur is present in oil compounds responsible for the characteristic odors of plants like garlic and onion. Never use more than 150 pounds per 1,000 square feet.

Sul-Po-Mag (or K-mag or sulfate of potash-magnesia): A mixture of K_2SO_4 and $MgSO_4$ used to provide potassium, magnesium, and sulfur nutrients to soils deficient in those elements. It is available in a synthetic and a natural form.

Superphosphate: The old-style superphosphate 0-18-0 or 0-20-0, made by treating rock phosphate with an equal amount of sulfuric acid, was a good source of phosphate in low-acid or high-alkaline soils because it became calcium sulfate and calcium phosphate, which are two products found in nature. However, little if any is still made. Triple superphosphate (0-46-0) is a more concentrated source of phosphorus. It is made by using phosphoric acid and is extremely destructive to soil fertility. It is so base that it quickly combines with various trace minerals, making them unavailable to plant roots.

Vermiculite: Soft shiny stuff in potting mixes, an alumino-silicate clay mineral similar to mica. It is mined and heated to 2,500°F, which causes it to expand into sterile, lightweight particles. It can hold 3–4 times its volume in water; it can also improve aeration and drainage of some soils and helps to hold cations (improves CEC, or Cation-Exchange Capacity) in some soils.

Vinegar: Vinegar is a wonderful organic tool that was discovered by accident ten thousand years ago when wine was accidentally allowed to ferment too long and turned sour. It can be made from many products, including beer, apples, berries, beets, corn, fruits, grains, honey, malt, maple syrup, melons, molasses, potatoes, rice, sorghum, and other foods containing sugar. Natural sugars from these food products are fermented into alcohol, which is then fermented into vinegar.

A strong vinegar available for general use is 20 percent or 200 grain, meaning that about 20 percent of the liquid is acetic acid. It is a petroleum-based product. At this strength, it is corrosive enough to eat metal and must be handled carefully in plastic containers. It is dangerous, and I don't recommend it. The weaker 100 grain (10 percent) works just about as well if used consistently, especially if orange oil is added at about 2 ounces per gallon. Since this diluting process cuts the cost in half, it's usually advisable to go ahead and use the weaker solution.

If your water is alkaline, add 1 tablespoon of 50-grain (5 percent) natural apple cider vinegar to each gallon of water to improve the quality of the water for potted plants and bedding. This doesn't have to be done with every watering, though it wouldn't hurt. This technique is especially helpful when trying to grow acid-loving plants such as gardenias, azaleas, and dogwoods. A tablespoon of vinegar per gallon added to the sprayer when foliar-feeding lawns, shrubs, flowers, and trees is also highly beneficial, especially where soil or water is alkaline. The other horticultural use for vinegar is the watering can.

Fruit vinegar is made from the fermentation of a variety of fruits. Apples are most commonly used, but grapes, peaches, berries, and other fruits also work. The product label will identify the starting ingredients, such as "apple cider vinegar" or "wine vinegar." Malt vinegar is made from the fermentation of barley malt or other cereal grains. Sugar vinegar is made from sugar, syrup, or molasses. White, spirit, or distilled vinegar is made by fermenting distilled alcohol. Distilled white vinegar is made from 190-proof alcohol that is fermented by adding sugar and living bacteria. Natural vinegar contains at least fifty trace minerals.

Wood Ash: Produced from the burning of wood. Becoming more available as more wood is being burned for energy production. It is a good source of plant nutrients if used in small amounts at one time. Wood ash is alkaline, and large amounts may affect the pH of the soil. Wood ash has been used for centuries as a source of plant nutrients.

Yucca Extract: Yucca extract not only makes sprays stick to crop foliage, it is also a great foliar material itself. It contains complex sugar structures that help plants assimilate nutrients and develop stress resistance.

Zeolites (aluminum silicates): Derived from ancient volcanic ash made of silicate minerals formed by the interaction of sea salt with molten lava, which creates a very interesting physical structure with lots of cavities and voids. They have the ability to absorb water even under dry conditions, or absorb huge amounts of gas or minerals and keep them readily available for plants. They are often used as cat litter, as they absorb odors, and in animal feed. When used as an amendment, they increase the CEC (Cation-Exchange Capacity) of soilless media. Over 48 types of zeolites with similar properties have been found in the United States. Zeolites have the ability to buffer and balance the chemistry of the soil. They will hold certain elements, such as ammonia, that are in excess and release them as biological activity develops.

Microbe Products

Products are now available that contain many species of beneficial soil bacteria. Some will pull nitrogen out of the air in soil and make it available to feed plants. When sufficient nitrogen-fixing bacteria is in the soil, the need for fertilizer is reduced. Other bacteria decompose organic matter and break down pesticides and other toxic residues in the soil. Soil bacteria reduce soil compaction by improving soil structure, creating microscopic spaces in the soil to hold air and water. Some soil bacteria attack and kill soil pathogens. Other products contain beneficial fungi that grow on the roots of plants, increasing the plants' ability to pull nutrients and water from the soil. Root growth is greatly enhanced when transplants and seed are exposed to the products prior to planting. These living products can also be applied to growing plants, but they have to get into the soil and have contact with the roots to work. Mycorrhizal fungi production works better in soils rich in organic matter with good structure and aeration. The best microbe products use a blend of bacteria and fungi. Examples of companies with these high-quality products include Bio-S.I., Mycorrhizal Applications, and Green Industries.

Micronized Products

Micronized products are made by mechanically pulverizing them into extremely fine texture. Properly micronized finished products have the consistency of talcum powder. The particles range in size from 5 microns to 75 microns. Their advantage is the tremendously enlarged surface area of the product, which enables plants to access the nutrients more efficiently. These products can be mixed dry into soil treatments or mixed with water and sprayed or drenched into the soil. This is an excellent choice when the use of compost tea would cause logistical problems. As the particle size gets smaller, the total surface area increases greatly. This allows more microbes to attack and dissolve the particles.

CHAPTER 6

Alternatives to Lawn Grasses and Turf

As this book was being planned, there was a fair amount of concern about whether to do a book that was positive about turfgrasses. Many homeowners would be surprised about that, since well-maintained lawns are an American tradition. The negativity came from people concerned about the idea of recommending the planting and maintenance of a crop that requires so much irrigation. Much of the South and especially much of Texas has suffered and is continuing to suffer from severe drought. There is no question that water is currently a major environmental and economic issue that will probably worsen with time.

Others were more concerned about feeding the world than about decoration and thought that food-crop plantings should be discussed, recommended, and used instead of lawns. Lawns are much better than bare soil with regard to cooling effects and preventing erosion, but turfgrasses can't be eaten. Fruits, vegetables, and herbs can be grown, and there is certainly more and more interest in growing food at home in order to know that it is clean. Maybe the emphasis and money spent ought to shift.

I agree that there are situations where turfgrass is not the most appropriate planting for the site. It definitely has to be admitted that more synthetic fertilizers and toxic pesticides are used on turf than on any other type of planting. On the other hand, there are easy-to-maintain and low-water-use turfgrasses that should be considered and used much more often than the commonly sold and planted St. Augustine, Bermuda, zoysia, and fescue. Take a look right here in this book, in chapter 2, at the information about the most practical turfgrass of all—buffalograss. It is the only American native turfgrass. It is also my favorite grass.

There are three basic situations where turfgrass should not be grown. The first is on property where there is simply more interest in growing food crops and other specialty plants. Fruit trees, vegetables, and herb crops can easily be grown in areas that get enough sunlight. Sunlight is the second issue. On many sites there isn't enough sunlight to grow turfgrass successfully. The third issue relates to water use. In most cases, there are crops that require less water than the commonly used turfgrasses.

Growing Alternative Crops and Specialty Plants

There are many options for alternatives to turfgrasses, depending on what part of the country you live in. They include herb gardens, vegetable gardens, edible flower gardens, butterfly gardens, and combinations of all the above. Edible landscaping can be designed so that there are fruits, vegetables, herbs, and other useful plants all mixed together. In fact, gardens can be designed that are 100 percent useful, with every plant in the garden having a use other than looking pretty. Vegetable gardens can sweep into beds that have more of a soft landscape appearance. Vegetable gardens do not have to look ugly or too utilitarian. There are edible landscaping plants, vegetable crops, and herbs that can be grown year-round. Here are a few of the many options for using edible crops in the landscape.

Summer Food Crops: Beans, beets, black-eyed peas, cardoon, chicory, climbing beans, cress, cucumbers, gourd, green beans, jicama, melons, peppers, snap beans, squash, tomatoes.

Fruits: Apples, figs, jujubes, peaches, pears, pecans, pomegranates, and various berries.

Cool-Season Crops: Arugula, cabbage, carrots, cauliflower, chicory, chives, endive, garlic chives, garlic, leeks, lettuce, mustard collards, onions, radicchio, sugar beets, sugar snap peas, Swiss chard, turnips.

Herb Gardens: Herbs can be designed for many different places and used instead of turf areas. The beds can also have a rectangular, formal appearance, or can be designed to have very soft, flowing lines. Many of the plants that we refer to as culinary or medicinal herbs are evergreen and have excellent landscaping value. In this category are bay, germander, rosemary, sweet myrtle, and so on. Others are perennial and have flowers for beauty as well as for attracting beneficial insects and various pollinators.

Edible Flower Gardens: Of course not all flowers are edible—some are poisonous either naturally or from toxic chemical pesticides. Only eat flowers grown organically. Flowers from florists, nurseries, and traditional garden centers should not be eaten. If your garden center is organic, eat away.

Eight Rules for Edible Flowers
1. Not all flowers are edible. Some are poisonous. Learn the difference.
2. Eat flowers only when you are positive they are edible and nontoxic.
3. Eat only flowers that have been grown organically.
4. Do not eat flowers from florists, nurseries, or garden centers unless you know they've been maintained organically.
5. Do not eat flowers if you have hay fever, asthma, or allergies.
6. Do not eat flowers growing on the side of the road.

7. Remove pistils and stamens from flowers before eating. Eat only the petals of the larger flowers.
8. Introduce flowers into your diet the way you would new foods to a baby—one at a time, in small quantities.

Notes: Pregnant women should avoid all strong herbs, and no plant should be ingested in excess by anyone at any time. None of these plants should be eaten unless they have been grown organically. Edible flowers can be used to enhance food at breakfast, lunch, and dinner. They can also be used in teas. Here are some of the best edible plant choices.

Shade Trees

Ginkgo—tea from leaves
Jujube—fruit
Linden—tea from flowers
Mulberry—fruit
Pecan—edible nuts
Persimmon—fruit
Walnut—edible nuts

Ornamental Trees

Apple—fruit and edible flower petals
Apricot—fruit and edible flower petals
Citrus—edible fruit
Crabapple—fruit and edible flower petals
Fig—fruit and edible flower petals
Mexican plum—fruit
Peach—fruit and edible flower petals
Pear—fruit and edible flower petals
Persimmon—fruit
Plum—fruit and edible flower petals
Redbud—edible flowers
Rusty blackhaw viburnum—edible berries
Witch hazel—tea from leaves

Shrubs

Agarita—fruit for wine
Althea—edible flowers
Bay—tea and food seasoning from leaves
Germander—freshens air indoors
Pomegranate—edible fruit
Turk's cap—flowers and fruit for tea

Annuals

Begonias—edible flowers
Daylilies—edible flowers
Dianthus—edible flowers
Ginger—food, seasoning, and tea from roots
Hibiscus—edible flowers
Johnny-jump-ups—edible flowers
Nasturtium—edible leaves and flowers
Pansies—edible flowers
Peanuts—edible nuts
Purslane—edible leaves
Sunflower—edible seeds and flower petals

Vines

Beans and Peas—edible pods and seeds
Gourds—dippers and bird houses
Grapes—food (fruit and leaves)
Luffa—edible flowers, shoots, and fruits; sponges from the dried fruit
Malabar spinach—edible foliage
Passion flower—edible fruit, tea from leaves

Ground Covers

Clover—tea from leaves and flowers
Creeping thyme—teas and food flavoring
Gotu kola—tea from leaves
Mints—food and teas from flowers and leaves
Oregano—teas and food flavoring
Violets—leaves in salads and tea from flowers and leaves

Perennials

Anise hyssop—edible flowers, foliage for tea
Blackberries—edible berries, foliage for tea
Chives—edible foliage and flowers
Garlic—edible flowers, greens, and cloves
Hibiscus—edible flowers
Hoja santa—leaves for cooking with meats
Horsemint—insect repellent
Jerusalem artichoke—roots for food
Lavender—teas and insect repellent
Monarda—edible flowers and leaves for teas

Peppers—edible fruit, tea from fruit
Purple coneflower—all plant parts for teas
Rosemary—food and tea from leaves and flowers
Roses—petals and hips for tea
Salvia—edible flowers, foliage for teas
Sweet marigold—food, flavoring, and tea from leaves and flowers
Tansy—chopped and crushed foliage repels ants
Turk's cap—flowers and fruit for tea

The Key to Successful Gardening Is Excellent Bed Preparation

The Don'ts

Don't remove native soil unless drainage problems are caused by the raised beds. Existing native soil is an important part of the bed-preparation mix.

Don't use peat moss, pine bark, or washed concrete sand. These products are problematic, especially when compared to the natural organic choices.

Don't till wet soil. Tilling, forking, or digging holes in wet soil does damage by squeezing the soil particles together, causing glazing and eliminating the air spaces needed for healthy soil life.

Don't spray toxic herbicides. Spraying toxic herbicides any time is a bad idea, but in the winter, it's really stupid because they can't kill dormant grasses and weeds.

Don't use any synthetic fertilizers. They salt up the soil and disturb or kill the beneficial life that helps roots develop.

The Dos

Remove unwanted vegetation wisely. Scrape away any existing weeds and grass and toss that material into the compost pile or replant the sod elsewhere. Always remove the grass before any tilling is done. Tilling first drives the reproductive part of the grasses and broadleaf plants down in the ground to be a weed problem forever. Organic herbicides such as the vinegar formula or the orange-oil products can be used in the summer, but physical removal is still better, especially if Bermudagrass is present. Some people recommend placing several layers of paper down over the grass, then adding soil on top of the paper to create the seed bed. I don't recommend that for several reasons. The most important is that burying living tissue creates an anaerobic condition and a black mulch layer that injures plant roots as they try to develop.

Raise the beds. Walls aren't essential, but the top of the beds should be flat and higher than the surrounding grades, with sloped edges for drainage. This lifting happens naturally if proper amounts of amendments are added to the native soil.

Add amendments. Use the existing native soil but add the following: 4–6 inches of compost, dry molasses or other organic fertilizer (2 lbs. per 100 sq. ft.), zeolite (10 lbs. per 100 sq. ft.), lava sand (10 lbs. per 100 sq. ft.), greensand (4 lbs. per 100 sq. ft.), and whole ground cornmeal (2 lbs. per 100 sq. ft.). If the budget allows, add ¹/₂ inch of decomposed granite. Rototill or fork to a total depth of 8 inches.

Moisten beds before planting. Planting beds should be moistened after being prepared and before the planting begins. They should be moist but not sopping wet. Do not plant in dry soil because the young roots will dehydrate quickly as they try to grow. The roots of any transplants should be sopping wet and thoroughly hydrated.

Plant bare-root plants. Pot-bound plants can resist water and cause deformed and unhealthy root development. Soak root balls in water for at least thirty minutes or until they are thoroughly saturated. Remove most if not all of the soil and synthetic fertilizer pellets. Spread the roots out in a naturally radiating position and then cover them with prepared bed soil. If you don't want to go the bare-root route, dip plant balls into water and install sopping wet root balls into moist beds. Add Garrett Juice and mycorrhizal fungi to the water for best results.

Plant high. Make sure the trunk flares are uncovered by removing excess soil. Set the plants high with the top of the root balls slightly higher than the surrounding soil and the trunk flare dramatically high and visible. This is especially critical on woody plants. Setting the plant too low can cause poor growth or drowning.

Mulch beds after planting. Add 2–3 inches of organic mulch after planting. Use shredded native tree trimmings for trees, shrubs, and ground cover, and a thinner layer of compost for annuals and perennials. Never pile mulch onto the stems of plants.

The shorthand explanation: Just add plenty of compost, rock minerals, and molasses to the native soil and mulch all bare soil after planting plants with thoroughly hydrated roots.

Low-Light Situations

A second reason not to grow turfgrass is when there isn't enough light. Grass can't grow in areas where the sunlight is too low because of trees or buildings or whatever is blocking the sunlight. It's actually one of the most common questions I get. Gardeners want to know how to add more fertilizer or change the amendments or do something so the grass can grow. The problem of growing grass in shade is that both the trees and the grass want sunlight, and guess which one wins that battle? So the only way to continue to grow grass in a shady situation is either to severely prune the trees or to remove them. Severely pruning the trees doesn't always work because the root system of the trees is also in competition for water and nutrients and is as big a problem as the canopy of the trees. Plus, overpruning deforms the trees and can severely affect their health. So what do we recommend in this case? We recommend planting a ground cover of some kind, and there are several choices. First of all, living ground covers can be planted, and in that category there are many options, including the following:

For Sun: Asian jasmine, creeping vinca minor, liriope, ophiopogon, purple winter creeper, sedum, thyme, Virginia creeper.
For Shade: Asian jasmine, Boston ivy, confederate jasmine, English ivy, gill ivy, liriope, ophiopogon, Persian ivy, Virginia creeper.

Another route to go in low-light areas is to use nonliving ground covers. In this category we have hard material such as gravels and organic mulches. The best gravels to use to cover a shaded area are lava gravel and decomposed granite. The biggest mistake made using this technique is putting plastic down first. Both "weed-blocking" fabrics and solid plastics foul up the soil surfaces, raise temperatures, interfere with and damage plant roots, and waste money. Mulches should be applied directly onto the bare soil, just as it works in the wild. There are several good natural mulch options: shredded hardwood, native tree trimmings, pine needles, and others. All of these alternative methods can be designed to blend with plants and be as attractive as turf or even better.

Water Concerns

The third reason not to grow turfgrasses is water use. Generally speaking, turfgrasses—with the exception of buffalograss—require more water than some alternative crops. Removing the grass or not planting it in the first place and preparing beds for other crops can certainly be considered. In some cases, it certainly should be. One of the slight negatives about this alternative approach is that soil preparation is much more important. See my bed preparation instructions above.

Xeriscaping

First of all, the word is not "zeroscaping," as many incorrectly say. This "technique" is often recommended as a water-saving approach. I always thought of it as a somewhat goofy term, but let's go with it here. Xeriscaping—or maybe a better term is "drought-tolerant landscaping"—is the use of practical planting techniques and drought-tolerant plants that require minimal amounts of irrigation. People who recommend this approach also tend to recommend drip irrigation, which to me is a major mistake in most landscape situations.

It is important to remember that there is no such thing as maintenance-free plants, even plants that are xeric or drought tolerant or so-called easy-to-maintain. For example, cacti, yucca, and similar plants still require certain levels of maintenance. They need some water, they need relatively decent bed preparation, they need to be planted in an area and exposure where they will grow well, and they need a modest amount of organic fertilizer.

The most important thing to learn about this issue is the dramatic water savings provided by a total natural organic program no matter what plants are used. The water savings afforded by switching to biological methods instead of the commonly used synthetic chemical program is in the 40–50 percent range. Unfortunately, many "xeriscape" projects still use synthetic chemicals and don't come close to saving the maximum amount of water.

Xeric Plant Lists

Some cities are now giving tax credits to homeowners who follow "xeriscaping principles." This primarily happens in cities that receive less than 9 inches of rain a year or something along those lines. Cities usually suggest acceptable drought-tolerant and xeriscape plants and sometimes even provide designs on websites to help the homeowners know how to proceed. It is unfortunate that not too many of these cities recommend organic techniques, which would give more significant water savings than anything else they could possibly do.

As pointed out in several places, there is no reason to ever use synthetic fertilizers no matter what plant or crop is being grown. Removal of synthetic fertilizers is the most significant change that can be made, and it can be done for turf, edible landscape or food crops, and xeriscape plants to reduce the amount of water used and the amount of water needed in the long term.

As I mentioned before, there are some very drought-tolerant grasses. Buffalograss is my personal favorite, but the following are some others.

Alternative Grasses to Lawn Grasses

Alkali grass (Puccinella distans): This grass is well suited for alkaline and salty soils in cool-season climates. It is used on golf course roughs or roadside reclamations where conditions are bad for the traditional lawn grasses. Alkali grass can get crowded out in acidic soils. For moist areas, this grass could be ideal. An improved cultivar from Colorado, 'Fults', is often used on lawns where the pH is above 7.5 and soil salts are high.

Blue grama (Bouteloua gracilis): This grass is native to the dry plains of central North America. It is highly drought tolerant, can grow to a foot or more, or can be mowed as a lawn grass. Considered a warm-season grass because it likes the hot weather and is slow to grow in spring, it is nonetheless hardy to Zone 3. Sometimes called mosquito grass because of the wispy appearance of its flower heads, it grows in clumps. It prefers heavy soils.

June grass (Koeleria macrantha): This is a native grass of the prairies and open woods of Canada and the United States. It is a drought-tolerant, cool-season species that requires little maintenance. It needs little to no fertilizer, occasional water, and almost no mowing. Cutting lower than 3 inches could be a problem and is not recommended. It may be used as a turf alternative, but because of its slow growth, a lawn would take years to fill in when planted by seeds.

Prairie dropseed (*Sporobolus heterolepsis*): This is an emerald-green, lush clumping grass. It is one of the most luxuriant cool-hardy prairie grasses for a sandy site. It is often used as an edging plant in perennial gardens where it can grow to 4 feet high. It can take high mowing in a low-maintenance lawn application. Native Americans use its seeds, which smell like cilantro, to grind into flour.

Prairie sandreed (*Calamovilfa longifolia*): This is a native grass used primarily for grazing and hay, but it can also be used as a warm-season lawn alternative, especially on sandy sites. It is very drought tolerant and able to withstand vast extremes in climate. Left to grow to its full potential, it extends to 5 feet tall with feathery flower heads.

Sheep fescue (*Festuca ovina*): This grass has many of the same tolerances to shade and drought as most fescues, but this one is a native and is especially well suited to sandy soils in cool-season areas and is one of the few grasses that grow in a gravelly site. It can be slow to get established.

The Lady Bird Johnson Wildflower Center in Austin, Texas, has formulated a multispecies mixture of native grass that works well in dry regions of Texas, Oklahoma, New Mexico, Arizona, and probably other parts of the country.

This mix idea resulted from research done at the Wildflower Center funded by Walmart. It was discovered that a mix of *Bouteloua dactyloides* (buffalograss), *Bouteloua gracilis* (blue grama), and *Hilaria belangeri* (curly-mesquite) work well together and need less mowing, watering, and weeding. These grasses have almost identically shaped leaves and color and produce attractive, even-textured, dense turf that does well in full sun but also tolerates about 50 percent shade. The mixes are available from native seed suppliers such as Douglass King Company and Native American Seed Company. The recommended seeding rate is about 3–4 pounds of Habiturf per 1,000 square feet.

The following are the soil preparation recommendations from the Wildflower Center:

A well-textured, well-drained soil is essential for long-term lawn success. Normally, after construction, developers spread a couple of inches of imported soil over soil compacted by heavy construction machinery. A sustainable lawn needs deep roots, so rip, rotovate, or disk your soil to at least 8 inches—the deeper the better. Then incorporate a ½-inch layer of living compost with a low nitrogen and low phosphorus content into the top 3 inches of your prepared soil. Ask your local plant nursery for recommendations. DO NOT use tree bark, wood shavings, or mulch. Grass won't grow in this. The soil surface should be finished to a fine granular texture and free from large stones. Note: If you are on undisturbed, uncompacted native soils, then till lightly and add ¼ inch of compost into the top 1 inch or, alternatively, add a compost tea.

I can go along with all that, but if this mix is as tough as it appears to be, it can grow in much worse conditions than explained above. If the budget allows, go ahead and create the much-improved conditions.

Here are their recommendations on sowing the seed:

To sow the seed, the small, hand-cranked seed broadcasters are great or by hand—and rake and press with a garden roller or your feet. Seeds need good soil contact. Spring is the best sowing time once soil temperatures warm up (daytime temperatures constantly above 85°F). Later in the growing season also works well but will require more water. Avoid sowing in late fall and winter (October through mid-March).

And on irrigation:

The lawn area should be irrigated every day for the first ten days or longer, up to fifteen days, under very hot, dry, or windy conditions to prevent the soil from drying out. Thereafter, two soil-wetting (top 4 inches of soil) events per week for the next month, then two soil-wetting (top 6 inches of soil minimum) events per month for the remainder of the growing season, which is March through November. Remove weeds as they appear, before they go to seed or become too established. Once the lawn is established in three to four months, you may opt to stop irrigating to save water and allow the lawn to go "drought dormant." The native grasses will go brown and temporarily stop growing but, adapted to drought, will green up once rain returns. In prolonged drought (say over six weeks in summer with no rain), an irrigation event (if allowed) once every five to six weeks, while not triggering "green-up," will keep the dormant turf alive.

All of this is good advice.

Management of this mix is easy once established. When mowed to about 4 inches, the native grass mix forms dense, fine-textured turf softer than common Bermudagrass or St. Augustine. Allowing the grass to seed out once a year produces a softer, longer appearance that some people like and allows the grasses to set seed, providing a seed bank for later use to cover areas damaged by drought, heavy foot traffic, weeds, and so forth. It also provides high habitat value. Natives are slower growing than St. Augustine and Bermudagrass and should be mowed less often. Irrigate with occasional deep-water events or hopefully rainfall, and maybe let this turf go dormant in summer.

This turf can be mowed at 3–4 inches for a good-looking, dense turf resistant to weeds and light to moderate foot traffic. A cut of 6 inches will produce a different look with a few seed heads if watered. Mow once every three to five weeks when growing and not at all when drought or cold dormant. Mowing shorter—2 inches or less—is okay, but not mowing at all through the growing season can produce a longer turf of 8 inches or so high with a lower density.

Make sure that the lawn overwinters as a thick, lush turf left at 4 inches high. This dramatically reduces the winter weeds the following spring—such as clover, dandelions, and rescuegrass. The last mowing should be a high 4 inches or so, and no later than mid-October.

Feeding should be kept to a minimum. Grass clippings left on the ground will be enough in most cases. Annual feeding should be the maximum ever needed. A healthy living soil plus the natural "rain" of airborne nutrients will be sufficient to keep your natural lawn balanced and not hungry. For high-use lawns with children and pets, or fast-draining soils, a fall dressing with a low-nutrient, living compost or Garrett Juice will help. Obviously, native grasses aren't synthetically fertilized. At least, they shouldn't be.

The bottom line is that homeowners will continue their love affairs with lawns, but there are several options to make grass growing more sustainable and responsible. The easiest part is to go organic and cut the irrigation costs in half. I hope this book gives you several other tips to help.

Differences between Toxic Chemical and Organic Approaches

Chemical Approach	Organic Approach
Mow low and often.	Mow higher and less often.
Catch grass clippings.	Leave clippings on the ground.
Apply high-analysis fertilizers 4–5 times per year.	Apply low-analysis fertilizers 2–3 times per year.
Use high-nitrogen fertilizers.	Use low-nitrogen fertilizers.
Uses synthetic fertilizer containing fillers but no organic matter.	Uses 100% organic fertilizer with no fillers.
Fertilizer chosen based on plant needs.	Fertilizer chosen based on soil needs.
Fertilizers used have few or no trace minerals.	Fertilizers used are loaded with trace minerals.
Attempts to control nature.	Attempts to work within nature's systems.
Treats symptoms (insects, diseases).	Treats soil and cultural problems.
Uses chemical pesticides at first sign of pests.	Uses natural pesticides but only as a last resort.
Poisons used on a calendar basis as preventatives.	Prevention through soil improvements and foliar fertilizers.
Discourages the use of beneficial insects.	Uses beneficial insects as a major tool.
Uses only university-tested products.	Uses food products, teas, and homemade mixtures where appropriate.
Damages soil health.	Improves soil health.

Formulas

Garrett Juice (Concentrate)

You can buy Garrett Juice commercially or you can make your own. The concentrate formula is as follows:

1 gallon compost tea or liquid humate
1 pint liquid seaweed
1 pint apple cider vinegar
1 pint molasses
Use 1½ cups of concentrate per gallon of water.

Garrett Juice (Ready to Use)

1 gallon water
1 cup compost tea
1 ounce liquid seaweed
1 ounce apple cider vinegar
1 ounce molasses

For Garrett Juice Plus, add 1 ounce of hydrolyzed fish. For Garrett Juice Pro, add beneficial bacteria and mycorrhizal fungi such as Bio-S-I. For added disease control, various organic pest-control products, such as orange oil, essential oils, and hydrogen peroxide, can be added.

Fire Ant Control Drench

Add 2–3 ounces of orange oil per gallon of the ready-to-use Garrett Juice formula.

Vinegar Herbicide

1 gallon full-strength vinegar (10%–20%)
2 ounces orange oil or d-limonene per gallon of vinegar
1 teaspoon liquid soap or other cleaning surfactant per gallon of vinegar

---

Unacceptable Fertilizer Products for Organic Projects

Ammonium nitrate	Ironite
Ammonium sulfate	Osmocote
Biosolids products	Peters 20-20-20
BR-61	Scotts Miracle-Gro products

Sewer sludge and biosolids products
SuperThrive
Synthetic growth regulators

Weed-and-feed fertilizers
Urea
All other synthetic fertilizers

Unacceptable Pest-Control Products for Organic Projects

2,4-D
Acetic Acid (petroleum based)
Amdro
Atrazine
Bayer products
Bayleton
BHA
BHT
Broadleaf herbicides
Clopyralid
Copper products
Daconil
Diazinon
DSMA
Dursban
Ethoxyquin
Finale
Fipronyl products
Funginex
Glyphosate products
Grazon
Ironite
Manage

Merit
MSMA
Orthene
Orthonex
Ortho products
PBO
Pendimethalin
Picloram
Piperonyl butoxide
Pyrethrin
Pyrethroid products
Pyrethrum
Rapid Gro
Rotenone
Roundup
Sabadilla
Silica gel
SU herbicides
Synthetic fungicides
Vinegars 20% and greater in strength
Vinegar made from glacial acetic acid
All other toxic synthetic products

Specific products that are approved by the Texas Organic Research Center (TORC) are listed in the Research section of www.dirtdoctor.com.

Index